PURE LUCK

Conceive, Believe, Achieve

The Extraordinary Life of
Paul Wattenberg

Paul at age 5, in 1936.

PURE LUCK

Conceive, Believe, Achieve

The Extraordinary Life of
Paul Wattenberg

Reminiscence Books
New York

Dear Katie – 10/18/2018
Thank you so much
for your visit –
May all your Dreams
And wishes all come
Congratulations on
those your Engagement –
Hugs – Paul Wattenberg

Pure Luck: Conceive, Believe, Achieve

Interviews conducted and edited by Teri Friedman, PhD
http://www.reminiscence-books.com
Cover and interior design by Katharine Gates

For information, please contact
Wendy Gottfried: wendy@gottfriedchannel.com

DEDICATION

I dedicate this book to my wife, Linda, my son, Lee, and my daughters, Debbie and Wendy. I want to thank Linda for her patience, caring and love during the past 52 years. Linda, you are my partner and best friend in life. A special thanks to my three children who have each individually made me so proud and blessed. Remember I am always there for you. I also dedicate this book to my grandchildren: Jamie, Ryan, Rachel, Cory, Kyle, Andrew, Ethan and Dylan. Each one is a very special blessing. I adore you and consider it a gift from God to have gotten to love and hug each one of you. May you always be close as a family.

I also would like to give a special thanks to my cousin, Frida Wattenberg, in Paris. She joined the resistance movement in France during World War II, and after the war became a historian, documenting the many stories and atrocities that sprung from that era. Through her invaluable research, she was able to provide me with many stories and, ultimately, the fates of several of our family members in Europe. I am deeply indebted to her.

I want to toast my very special family with these very special words: "May you always have love to share, health to spare and friends that care."

I love you all. ✴

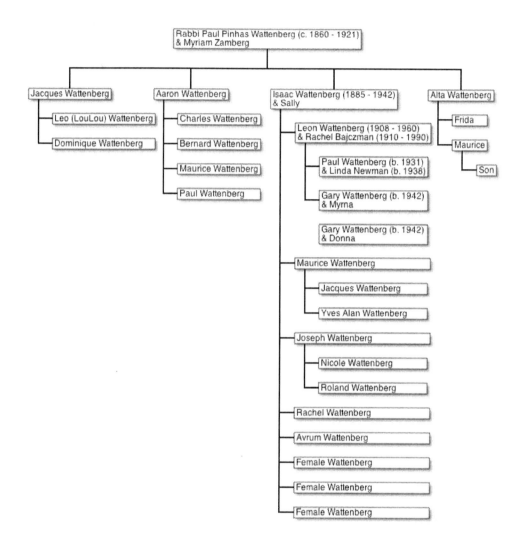

REFLECTION

As I have read many books and autobiographies about people who survived the atrocities, murder, and gassing which occurred during the Holocaust, I have realized how blessed and lucky my mom and I were to have escaped from the most horrendous genocide that has ever occurred in mankind – six million innocent men, women and children were massacred and murdered just for being of the Jewish faith. I have written this memoir so future generations will not forget that the Holocaust did occur. May this horrendous chapter never be repeated. As humans on earth, let us all respect each other's religious faiths. God bless the United States of America. ✱

TABLE OF CONTENTS

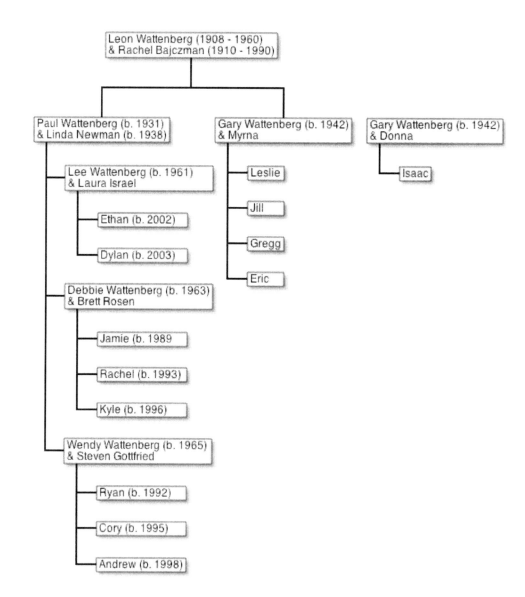

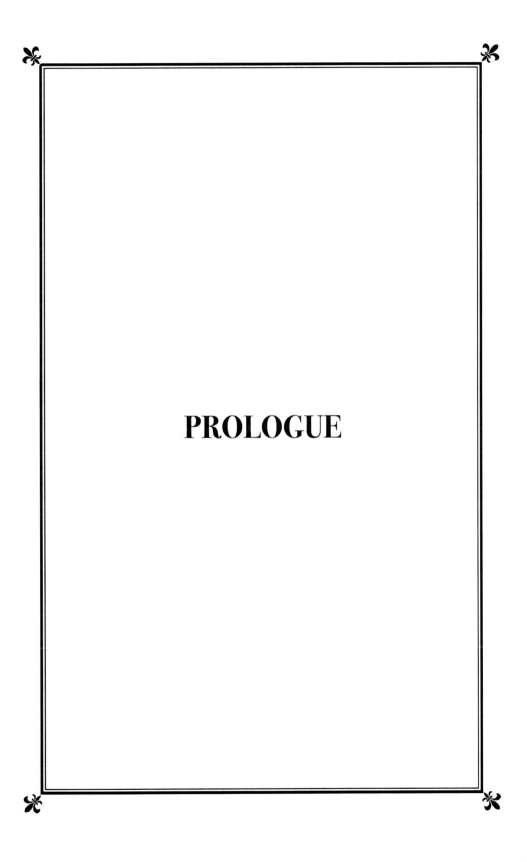

PROLOGUE

My life is very surreal. There is my "life before" and my "life after," sort of like before-Christ and after-Christ. I once had a huge family – great-grandmothers, grandmothers, grandfathers, aunts, uncles, girl cousins, boy cousins – some in Poland, some in France. My father was the eldest of nine children. My mother was one of seven. With very few exceptions, this beautiful family was completely destroyed in the Holocaust. Some died in Auschwitz/Berkinau and Treblinka. Some were just machine-gunned down in the street. My father's mother was killed near her home. On my mom's side, her mother Sally, her older sister Eva, and her baby brother Itche were also brutally murdered, some in Auschwitz, some in their own hometown.

My compulsion to go to Auschwitz/Berkinau was finally made a reality in September, 2007. I needed to breathe the air and see with my own eyes where many of my family members were slaughtered. I will later express my feelings and emotions regarding the Nazi bestiality and their unbelievable, methodical mass murder. As I reflect upon such genocide and how it came to pass that six million babies, children, men and women were methodically liquidated in Europe between 1939 and 1945, I realize that words can never truly express, nor give reason as to why and how human beings could be so cruel to other human beings because they were of a (Jewish) religion. After all, these Jewish people were human beings with families, hearts, souls, emotions, blood and arteries, tears and a zest for life. Yet, all became victims of the Holocaust.

All were murdered.

My family perished between 1942 and 1945. Fortunately, there were a few survivors among my relatives, whom we discovered after the war. I will talk about them later in my story.

My mother, my father, and I survived. We came to America and started a new life, a new family. My baby brother, Gary, born in 1942 in

Prologue

the United States, never knew the "before" family. But although he never experienced them as living souls, many of their stories were repeated to him time and time again and he became very cognizant of the Holocaust tragedy. To me, the family, their stories, are living memories. I remember and love them now, just as I did back then.

For fifty-five years, people have asked me the same questions that I have asked myself: How did I escape? Why did I get away? Why didn't the other people?

There are two answers which, I believe, dwarf all others. The first answer is my mother's extraordinary tenacity and courage, which really bordered on super-human. The other answer is luck, pure and simple. You can be smart, you can be bright, you can be brilliant, but at the end of the day, with no *mazel*, (luck), it doesn't fly. That is the whole story of life. It is the story of my life. ✶

Two years old, 1933.

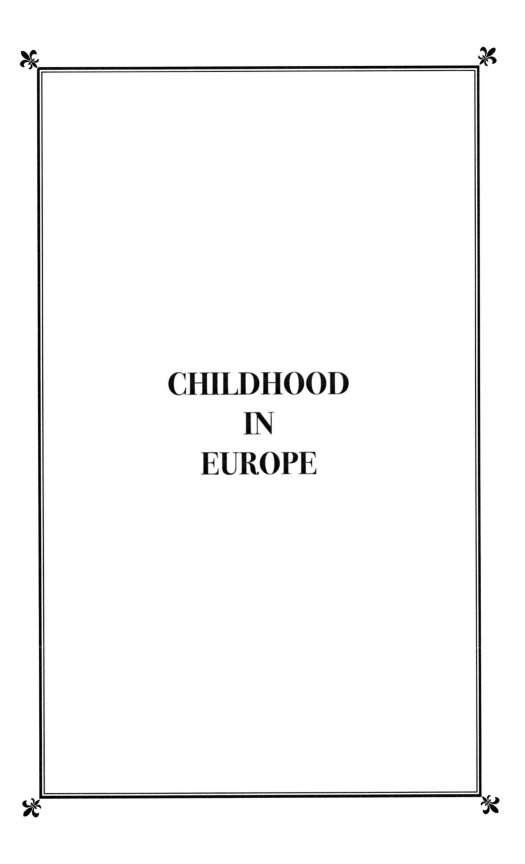

CHILDHOOD
IN
EUROPE

KP 99455

Préfecture du Département de la Seine

EXTRAIT ... du ... ... de NAISSANCE

du 20ᵐ Arrondissement de Paris

Le vingt-neuf avril mil neuf cent trente-et-un ,
vingt-et-une heures, est né rue Orfila 110, Paul,
du sexe masculin, de Léon WATTENBERG, né à Pamasz...
we (Pologne) le .....mil neuf cent huit, tailleur,
et de Ruchla BAJEZMAN, née à Radom (Pologne) le
.....mil neuf cent dix, sans profession, son époux...
domiciliés à Paris, 24 rue de la Butte aux Cailles.
EN MARGE EST ECRIT: Reconnu à Paris, treizième ar
rondissement, le vingt-et-un ao ut mil neuf cent
trente-trois, par Léon WATENBERG et par Ruchla 4 4
BAJEZMAN .- Pour extrait conforme: Paris, le premi...
septembre mil neuf cent trente-trois,/.J

... le maire:

My birth certificate.

I was born on April 29th, 1931 in Paris, France. I have my original birth certificate. Translated from the French, it reads:

> April 29th, 1931, at the 21st hour. Born on Rue de Feuille, male, to Léon Wattenberg, born in Tomaszow-mazovietsky in Poland, 1908, April 10th, tailor. Rachel Bajczman, born Radom, Poland, May 15, 1910. With no profession, housewife. Living at 24 Rue Butte Aux Cailles, officially in Paris, 13th district, 21st, issued birth certificate August, 1933.

My father didn't get my birth certificate until two years after I was born. I think my mother must have bugged him, "Why didn't you get the birth certificate?"

Eventually, he got it.

Family Background

I always wondered how they chose my first name. It turns out to be the name of my paternal great-grandfather, Rabbi Paul Wattenberg, who did not have a congregation but was learned in Talmud. He was born in Poland, in a small town called Tomaszow-mazovietsky, not far from Lodz, which is a very famous industrial, textile center in Poland, known for its production of wool. Born in about 1860, he died about ten years before I was born. Paul had three sons, Jacques, Isaac and Aaron, and one daughter, Alta.

One of Paul's sons, Isaac, was my grandfather. Isaac married a woman named Sally and they had ten children. My father, Leon, was the eldest. Isaac Wattenberg was Orthodox and a cantor. He had an operatic voice. Since his father was a rabbi, they studied Torah (Old Testament of the Bible) day and night, night and day, and they were not focused on making a living. Torah was most important. They had a little house that sheltered ten children and the parents in four rooms. But my grandfather was also an entrepreneurial type who knew how to bake. He owned two bakeries in town which sold fresh bread. He was president of the Baker's Association in Tomaszow. The five daughters worked in the bakery. The sons helped as well, in addition to being religious and studying Torah. They had a stand in the public square and on Sundays, they sold bread at the market in town. As a baking family, they could make a few dollars (*zlotys* in Polish currency) and live reasonably well in that particular era.

I knew my mom's mother. I also knew both my grandparents on my father's side. I was the only grandchild they ever knew because they were killed in the Holocaust before the other grandchildren were born. But that's getting ahead of my story.

My father, Leon, was born on April 20, 1908. As a boy, Leon was a very talented violinist. He won a prize in 1925 for his violin playing when he was 16 years old. As part of that prize, which was sponsored by the Zionist organization, he won a trip to Israel, which was called Palestine at the time. He traveled from Poland to Palestine and worked on a kibbutz, tilling the land, trying to make vegetables from sand. He was one of the original Zionist pioneers. He must have committed to stay, but then, as now, the Arabs were looking to kill the Jews. One of his close friends at the kibbutz got in the way of an Arab bullet and was blinded in one eye. The chief of the kibbutz asked for a volunteer, *Who will take this wounded gentleman to Paris to see an eye surgeon?* It was the only place in Europe where they knew there was a chance to save his eyesight. My father volunteered and went with his friend to Paris. They did the surgery

My paternal great-grandparents,
Paul (Pinchas) and Muriam Wattenberg.

My paternal grandparents,
Isaac and Sally Wattenberg, 1908.

My maternal grandparents,
Perl and Gershon Bajczman, c. 1935.

My father Leon and his mother Sally,
Tomaszow, Poland, 1927.

and his friend's eyesight was restored. While in Paris, my father met up with one of his father's oldest brothers, his Uncle Jack Wattenberg. Jack was living there, having migrated around 1920. My father didn't return to Palestine with his friend. I guess with all the shooting and suffering there, he chose to stay in Paris.

When my father started his career in Paris, he was working for his Uncle Jack doing carpentry. He didn't like it. He worked very hard, around the clock. As he related it to me, not only was he doing the carpentry, but he had to deliver the finished furniture. In those days, there were basically no trucks. To make a delivery, you had a horse and cart if you were a successful operation. Otherwise, and this was my father's case, you had to get a wheelbarrow type of contraption and *schlep* (carry) it all over town, delivering the furniture. He said that after doing this for a year, his back was hurting him.

After a couple of years, he decided to give up carpentry. He became an apprentice and learned how to custom design men's and ladies' suits.

Just as in this country, in Paris they had people coming in from foreign lands. Among the Jewish community they had groups they called *chavurim* – reunions, or communities, of friends from the "old country." If someone came from your community, let's say it was Warsaw, then all the other people from Warsaw were your *landsmen*. They would have a dance or a get-together, a place to congregate, to socialize a little, drink some wine. My father used to go with his friends from Tomaszow-mazovietsky to these informal gatherings.

My mother, whose maiden name was Rachel Bajczman, was living with her brother Hersh in Paris, but she, too, was originally from Poland. She was born on May 15, 1910. The town she grew up in was called Radom. In Paris, she had her group of friends from Radom. I guess the various Polish communities gravitated toward each other because they all spoke Polish. Nobody spoke French. Both my mother and father attended a gathering, and it was there that they met. She was 18 years old. He was 20.

My parents had the common bond of being familiar with the tailoring trade. My mother's father was a *couturier* in Poland, making ladies' coats. Coats were all made-to-order in those days. My mother helped her father with the tailoring. My father also had experience as a tailor. I am guestimating that he learned it in Palestine and in Paris. They got married in 1930. After they married, they opened up a custom tailoring store for men and women. We lived in the back of the store. It was called *Maison Léon* (House of Leon), at 24 Rue Butte aux Caille (Street of Pigeons).

My father Leon, 19 years old. Paris, 1927.

Uncle Maurice holding me, with my father's cousin, my father and my mother. In front of *Maison Léon*, Paris 1933.

I actually went with my kids to visit that store in Paris several years ago. It had become a grocery store. I described it to them as I recalled it. I said, "You're going to be in shock when you go inside. You'll see a skylight in the back. The mice used to run right across it."

We walked in. This was 50 years later. The same skylight was there. So was the bathroom in the courtyard outdoors. It was very emotional. It all looked so small.

When I was born in 1931, my father was still struggling to make a living. Tailoring, in those days, was a "cottage industry." The work was all done for individual customers by individual tailors. The tailor would take the measurements, bring the material home and make the garment. He would probably work with his wife and, if he had a couple of children, they would help him. He'd have a couple of sewing machines, a pressing iron, some lights. If he was more adventurous, maybe he'd hire an assistant to work with him, and pay him or her per garment.

The problem was, as a custom tailor, you needed fabric and linings and buttons to make clothes to order. In those days, you had to pay cash. My father was really a very poor man just starting out in the world. Nobody trusted him to give him two meters of fabric on credit. After all, who was this person? They didn't know him. One day by chance, he bought a lotto ticket, just like we do today.

Guess what? He won the lottery!

Pure luck!

His name appeared in the paper: *Léon Wattenberg Won the Lotto.* He probably won about $1000. But in the paper, they didn't specify the amount. People right away assumed, *God knows how much money he's got!* Suddenly, every supplier offered him goods without pay. *Take what you want, Léon. Take the whole piece, 50 meters! Take 30 meters! You don't have to pay me. Don't worry. Your credit is good!* Before they wouldn't give him two meters of material to make a blazer or suit. Now they gave him whatever he wanted.

All of a sudden, he thought, "I have too much fabric. What am I going to do with it?"

He started making a few garments that he decided to sell to other stores. *Look, why don't you take in a few ready-made garments?* That's how he went into the wholesale business. He continued custom–made tailoring, but his business really thrived when he went into ready-to-wear manufacturing. He was one of the early men's clothing manufacturers in France. Of course, manufacturing wasn't done on a mass production scale like it is today. My father, with some cutting assistants he hired, would cut the garments. He had a few tailors doing the rest of the work. Within five years, he was very successful.

Middle row, seated: Aunt Toby, my father, my mother.
Front row: Cousin Betty, myself and unknown boy. Deauville, France, 1933.

My mother, father and me on vacation, 1935.

My father and me with our Renault. Paris, 1935.

My father, me and mother (in short white jacket) in our new Citroën, 1937.

Wedding of Uncle Maurice and Aida Wattenberg, Paris, 1939. My father is at the far left. My grandfather Isaac is at the far right, with me standing in front of him and my mother next to him.

Vacation in Biarritz, France, 1934. Aunt Loly and Uncle Itche on left,
Aunt Toby in flowered dress, my mother and father standing, right.
In the bottom row, my cousin Betty is in the middle and I am on the right.

We started taking vacations. I have a photograph of us in 1934 in
Biarritz, which is on the Atlantic Coast, towards Spain.

In 1936, my father decided to take us to Poland to visit his family.
With his French passport, he figured he was safe. Don't forget, he'd migrated when he was 16, and hadn't been home in 12 years.

He had no idea what he was getting into. We were going to have to
pass through Germany to get from Paris to Tomaszow, Poland. A friend
of his who had knowledge of politics thought the trip was dangerous.

To help us out, the friend said, "You know what? I'm connected with
the French government. Why don't you put a French flag on the front of
your car? You will give the appearance of being a French diplomat."

We were driving through Germany and to me, a five year old boy,
it felt like we were never going to sleep. I said, "Gee, aren't we going to
go to sleep?"

My father and me with our Citroën. Tomaszow, Poland, 1936.

We stopped at a hotel in Leipzig, Germany. My father went to register and the man showed him a sign: *No Dogs, No Jews*. My father came back out. He said nothing. When we got to Poland, he told his father about the sign. He just couldn't believe it. There was already a certain discomfort brewing in the air.

Our arrival in my father's Citroën in Tomaszow was an unforgettable moment since it was a very triumphant return. Here was Leon Wattenberg, who left home at 16 years of age with a violin and a few clothes, one valise, and several *zlotys* (dollars). However, he had one great, invaluable asset — his vision, passion, optimism and spirit to try to make a better life and escape from the poverty. Tomaszow had a very small population. Besides the entire family of Wattenbergs, about 200 people greeted us as we arrived. They lined the entrance to the city. Our seven-seater Citroën was a type of car never seen in this small Polish town. I recall my Grandfather Isaac built a shed in the backyard to act as a garage cover. However, the car was twice the size of the shed! We stayed in Poland for two weeks. I got to know uncles, aunts, and cousins whom I had never met. My father's youngest brother Avrum (my uncle) was about 10 years old. We became playmates. My recollection of the family is that there were at least over 70 immediate family members that I got to know. We then went to Radom to meet my mother's mother, her sisters, brothers, and many cousins. I was in awe of the whole family. They were religious, humble, poor people. However, the warmth and love of family was something which became permanently instilled in me. Family togetherness and bonding was, and is, supreme.

My father's brother Morris (Maurice) was already living in Paris, where he lived with us and worked. The family wanted another brother,

l to r: Me, my father, my mother is fifth from left. Tomaszow, Poland, 1936.

Joseph, to come over, too. During our visit to Poland, my father made a secret plan for Joseph, which he implemented when we were back in Paris. Joseph and my dad looked like twins, even though my father was four years older. My father sent Joseph his French passport which, of course, included his picture, along with a train ticket. Joseph passed the German lines by showing my father's passport which "proved" he was from Paris. They looked at the passport, they looked at him, and they let him through. That was how Joseph got to Paris.

My father had a master plan. He was going to bring the whole family to Paris. He was going to pay for their transport, their housing, and everything else because he was so financially successful. His parents talked amongst themselves and a plan was formulated. They couldn't all go at once. They thought to bring my grandfather over, get him set up in an

Reception by family and villagers upon our arrival in my father's hometown of Tomaszow-maziovetsky, Poland, 1936. We are in my grandfather's backyard.
1. Grandpa Isaac; 2. Grandma Sally; 3. My mother's sister, Toby; 4. My mother's mother, Perl; 5. My mom, Rachel; 6. My father's brother, Avrum; 7. My father's sister; 8. My father's brother, Joseph; 9. My cousin, Betty Milgram; 10. Me, 5 years old, on my father's (11) knee.

apartment, and then bring the others. But my grandfather was very Orthodox and kosher, as was his whole family. He said, "How are we going to do this? How am I going to survive in Paris without my wife?"

His wife said, "Don't worry about me. Why don't you go to Paris with our daughter, Rachel? Leon, Morris, and Joseph are already there. Once you get there, the other girls, Avrum and I will make arrangements to come six months later."

The reason my grandmother suggested Rachel go was that Rachel was an excellent cook. She cooked kosher, which was just what my grandfather needed.

So that was the plan. In 1938, just before *Krystallnacht*, they were able to obtain a visa for my grandfather and his daughter, Rachel. Luck!

Passover, Paris France 1938.
Standing: Uncle Joseph, Uncle Maurice, Great-Aunt Bertha (wife of Jack), Aunt Rachel (my father's eldest sister). Seated: Me (7 years old), my mother, Grandfather Isaac, Great-Uncle Jack (Isaac's brother), my father.

My mother Rachel seated in center at 17 years old. Radom, Poland, 1927.

Wattenberg family, Tomaszow-Maziovetsky, Poland. August, 1936. L to r: top row: One of my father's sisters, my father, his sister Rachel, brother Maurice, another sister. Middle row: My father's brother Joseph, his mother Sally, me (5 years old), my mother Rachel, my grandfather (Dad's father) Isaac. Bottom row: My father's sister and brother.

They came to Paris and moved into an apartment procured for them by my father at 36 rue de Lancry, Paris X'ième.

Then *Krystallnacht* occurred. This was the night when the Nazis burned synagogues and shattered, destroyed, and ultimately closed many Jewish stores and businesses. It was the start of the genocide. At this point, the doors out of the country slammed shut. Jews were no longer able to get visas for France.

My grandmother and the rest of the family were not able to get out.

My Father Leaves for America

In Paris, my father had a very good friend by the name of Slivovsky. He was a very bright man who worked in the French government. He had intimations that Hitler was way out of hand. He said to my father, "They have the World's Fair in Queens, New York. Why don't you and I go to the World's Fair? If you have a few dollars, bring them with you. Maybe you can open a business there."

That discussion took place in June, 1939. In July, for vacation, we rented a cottage in the French Riviera with the Slivovsky family. I played with their son and daughter. Upon our return to Paris, my father and Mr. Slivovsky made arrangements to go to America. They left on August 19th or 20th from Le Havre on *The Normandy*, which was the first luxury ship built by the French. It was the premier steamship in the world at that time, as well as the fastest. The trip took five or six days. The plan was to go to America for two weeks. It never occurred to me that I might not see my father again, at least not for several years.

On August 27th, 1939, Hitler attacked Poland. As its allies, England and France had an agreement with Poland, that if Hitler attacked, they would all act as one. So in retaliation for Hitler's aggressive assault on

My father's passport photo to leave France
for the United States.

My father in Paris, 1938.

Poland, France and England declared war on Germany. This was the beginning of World War II. All this craziness happened seven days after my father set sail for America. Talk about luck.

Two weeks later, my father received a draft notice from the French army in Paris. My mother sent him a cable and he replied, *I'm coming back. I'm not staying here.*

My mother replied in another cablegram, *Please. Please! Your brothers Joseph and Morris were just inducted in the French army. Why are you coming back? Paul and I are going to try to go to Spain with your father and your sister, Rachel.*

So that's how my father got to America. Ultimately, it was Mr. Slivovsky who was indirectly responsible for us escaping because, had he not had the foresight to take my father to America with a few dollars to try to open a business, my father wouldn't have been here. If he weren't here, my mother and I would never have gotten our visas to come to the United States.

Luckily, my father had money in dollars, so he was able to go into business in New York. He worked for someone else for about six months in order to learn the ropes. He became fluent in the language. He opened a company on 14th Street which he called *Léon of Paris* in 1941, which was after we had already gotten our visas to come. He wasn't really concentrating on business, but he had to make a living. After all, how much money could he have brought over? He had taken gold bars with him. In those days, the old-fashioned thinking was not to take money, but gold. Gold was the standard and people trusted it because there were lots of currency fluctuations.

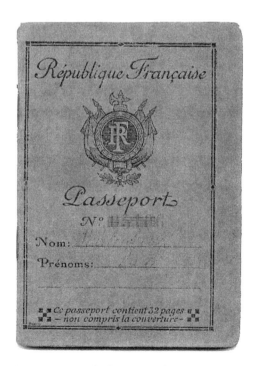

My passport, used when we tried to escape France
but were caught on June 16, 1940.

Attempted Escape, Captured

We were back in Paris and the Germans were attacking France. They had penetrated the Maginot Line, a military boundary that the French had built along the border of Germany and France. Along this border, the French had built a wall with gun turrets, with the guns facing Germany. There were land mines and 10,000 French troops guarding the Line. It was believed to be an area of impossible penetration. Everybody believed France was safe. In Paris, my mother would always tell me, "Don't worry. We have the Maginot Line. The Germans will never get here. We're safe."

What did the Germans do? They declared war on Belgium and went through Belgium to get to France. They were maybe 100,000 strong. The stupid thing is that when the French built the guns on the Maginot Line, they built them so that the guns couldn't be turned around. They could only face Germany. When the Germans came into France from Belgium, they circumvented the Line completely, and attacked France from within its own borders. They destroyed the entire French garrison of 10,000 soldiers. Once they destroyed the Maginot Line, they were able to cross over directly from Germany. Paris became completely vulnerable.

They were maybe 100 miles out of Paris. My Uncles Joe and Morris were in the French army, and they advised us to try to run for our lives. They said the German war machine was very strong and was destroying the French army. They said we should make an attempt to go to Spain or Portugal, which were thought to be neutral. Nobody knew they were in collaboration with Germany. So we set out to escape. I'll never forget the date: June 10, 1940. I was nine and my mother was 30 years old.

I remember my mother trying to decide what to bring. She took all the family photo albums of me when I was a child. That was what was

My passport, used when we tried unsuccessfully to escape France in 1940.

most special to her. She put the albums in the trunk of our Citroën. She also packed in some clothes, blankets, water, and cans of food.

We were five or six of us together in one car: my mother; her sister Tobi; Tobi's daughter Betty; my father's father, Isaac; and myself. I don't remember if Isaac's daughter, Rachel, was with us – she might have been. My mother's brother-in-law, Chuna, went with two other people because we thought it would be safer to split up – we already had too many people in one car. The Germans were approaching and they were killing everyone in sight.

We left Paris in our car with the intention of driving to Spain. It was total chaos. Just imagine, living in New York, fifteen million people on the FDR Drive and the West Side Highway, trying to get to New Jersey or maybe north to Canada. People were panicked. The roads were clogged. Traffic was not moving. It was bumper to bumper. There was no gas, no pumps, no electricity. Overhead, German planes were periodically dropping bombs and strafing targets on the ground.

Even though we had money, it didn't help, because if there is no gas, there is no gas. There was no food, no nothing. And I was a very, very skinny kid. I was unbelievably hungry. The little bit of rations we had were gone.

My mother was desperate for food, not for herself, but for me and my cousin Betty. She saw that I was starving and getting weak. She saw someone like an army captain, approached him and said, "Monsieur, Monsieur, please, we need some food. Can we get a potato? Can we get anything?"

He said, "Go down to the end of the road. They are cooking potatoes."

I remember this because it was very scary. I was tired. It was late in the evening. She said to the others, "I'm going to go get some potatoes. The French army is making some potatoes."

She went with her sister to the army post where they managed to get three or four potatoes and bring them back. I think it was a rainy night. I vividly remember my hunger. My mother gave me half a potato, which was cooked, and it fell into the mud. I was so hungry that I just wiped off the mud and ate it.

My cousin Betty remembers a slightly different version of this story. She remembers our mothers went to a French army post where they were cooking noodles and begged some from the soldiers. But we didn't have the equipment to warm up the noodles, so she said our mothers found an old rusty pot. Somehow they got water. She says it tasted disgusting, but we ate. Noodles or potatoes — what does it matter? We were starving.

The scary part of that story is that the building my mother went into to get the food was bombed about eight to ten minutes later. She could have been killed right then and there.

So many little things happened that were crazy and scary.

My mother was driving. She had just gotten her license and this was her first time really driving, so it was a helluva mess. We had enough gas for a couple of days. We may have picked up some more along the way but, eventually, we were completely out. We didn't want to just leave the car in the middle of the road, so my mother decided it would be most advantageous to look for a local farm. We were somewhere near the Atlantic Ocean, between Paris and Spain. We pulled into a farmhouse. She went to the farmer and asked him if she could leave the car there for safekeeping. She gave him some money, probably comparable to a couple of hundred dollars. She asked him if he would guard the car.

"No problem," he said. "Leave it here, give me the keys and I'll take care of it."

Perhaps naïvely, my mother thought she could trust this farmer. In truth, she had no other choice.

I remember that incident quite vividly because the car belonged to my father and I asked, "Why are you leaving the car? Why?"

I was nine years old and I didn't want to leave it behind. But, of course, we had to. We took some clothes, but we had no choice but to leave behind most of the stuff that was in the trunk, including our photo albums.

We started to walk to Spain, which was about 600 miles away. We were walking along the same road we had been driving on. It was much quicker to walk because of the congestion and the craziness of wartime. Army personnel were also running away, trying to escape along with the civilian population. It was total chaos. It was in the country, so we slept on the grass at night. I think my mother had a blanket. We did the best we could with what we had. We didn't have much food. We walked a day, maybe a day and a half, but it wasn't really working. After all, along with my mother and her sister, we were a nine year boy, a ten year old girl, and my grandfather who was in his mid–fifties. Progress was very slow. How many miles could you walk in a day? If you had to go 600 miles, it could take two months. At that point, my mother made other arrangements.

Through luck or money, my mother was able to get a guy who had a truck. The truck must have been about 20 feet long. There was enough room in the back for all of us to get in with our blankets and the couple of things we had taken along. Even in the truck, it was very slow-going. German airplanes, giant machine-gunners called *messerschmidts*, which were the state-of-the-art aircraft at the time, were strafing the ground, trying to kill French soldiers. As a civilian, you didn't want to get caught in the cross-fire. So every time they were somewhere near us, we'd hop out of the truck to run into the woods and hide. We did not want to be targets.

As a nine year old boy, I must admit that it was all very exciting, stupid as that may sound now. I was naïve to the danger. I remember hiding in the woods when a German plane flew above us and began strafing the ground with machine-gun bullets. I wanted to see the plane, so I stood up. This was contrary to what we had been told, which was to keep our heads down and stay as close to the ground as possible. My cousin, Betty, felt the same excitement. She remembers her mother telling her to stop looking at the airplanes. To us, it was fascinating. Luckily, we didn't get hit. Again, when I think about how we managed to survive the whole war, I attribute it to a lot of luck.

We spent six days on this attempted escape. In all that time, I don't think we even got 200 miles outside of Paris. We had given up the car, then walked, then arranged for the truck, but we still had to constantly run out and hide. Our movement was virtually paralyzed.

I will always vividly remember the night we were captured by the Germans. We were in the truck and it was nighttime. We had driven into the woods, probably along some kind of corridor or path. It was ten or eleven at night and the driver, too, had to get some sleep. We figured we'd all get a little shuteye for a few hours and continue on the road in the morning. I think I was the only one who was still awake when I saw a flash with very bright lights: German troopers. We had not realized when we pulled off the road that we were in the same location as French army troops, who were in hiding. The Germans, on the other hand, were very aware of the French army's whereabouts. It was strictly a coincidence that we pulled off into their exact location. When they flashed those lights on, it must have been about 2:00 or 3:00 in the morning. From pitch black, we were suddenly bathed in floodlights.

We heard them issue an ultimatum to the French army. *We have you surrounded. You will surrender* – white flag in the air or whatever – *otherwise, we will bring in our planes. This is your option. Either surrender or be killed.*

The French surrendered, at least that particular segment of the army. The war, of course, didn't end. But on that particular night, that group, maybe a couple of thousand soldiers who were hiding in the forest, they surrendered. I guess the commander said, "Look, we're surrounded. If we fight, we'll all get killed." Not knowing what lay in store, he must have figured it was better to be prisoners-of-war.

I saw all that, although I didn't really understand at the time that the French army was being captured. I remember that the Germans – this was in 1940 – had the best uniforms. They had the most amazing raincoats and the most amazing hats and motorcycles and state-of-the-art armored vehicles. They were at their peak. We didn't know what was really happening. Nobody knew at the time, the whole craziness about creating concentration camps and killing Jews. I don't even think the plan had been formulated yet.

The war was still in its beginning stages. The Germans were trying to get France to collaborate. The French government and Hitler signed an armistice. Armistice – they surrendered! So rather than killing everyone on sight, as they had been doing previously, the Germans were now trying to be very nice. While the five of us were still standing in the woods, they made an announcement, which I realized years later was for propaganda purposes. They invited all the children to get on line and announced they were going to give us chocolate and milk. They knew the children hadn't been eating.

I said, "Maybe I'll go get some chocolate."

My grandfather said, "No, I don't want you to go."

That I remember. He was very concerned, very scared – who knew what the Germans had in mind? But they did exactly as they said. They gave out milk and chocolate, while they filmed the whole scene. They had regular *ciné* film, news-type film, that they planned to use as propaganda to show the whole world, *See? We're nice people. We captured the French army, but we gave the children milk, we gave them chocolate. Here they are eating it.*

I was very upset about not being allowed to join in — it was just chocolate, what was the big deal? Of course, my grandfather was right.

They told us they were in the midst of making some kind of peace arrangement with Petain's Vichy government. They requested that everybody return to their homes. All the able-bodied men from the French army were made prisoners-of-war. But the civilians like my family, they told us to go back to Paris.

So we were captured. They wouldn't let us just continue to travel on — that phase was over. But they were generally nice, not inhuman. At that moment, I would say they were reasonable. They advised us to return to Paris and register, but their attitude, I would say, was very laissez-faire.

My mother must have given the truck driver some money and he drove us back to Paris.

Return to Paris, under German Occupation

Back in Paris, they wanted to register where we lived. They were probably formulating the beginnings of a master plan. Think about it. If you want to murder one person, you get a hit man, he kills the guy and that's the end of it. But if you want to kill ten million — there were ten million Jews in Europe — you've got to have a plan. First of all, you've got to know where the people are. How are you going to know where they are unless you have their addresses? Where do they live? How many people are in each apartment? What floor are they on?

We went back to Paris and my mother registered.

When we first got back into our apartment, it was a shock. We had a very large, beautifully furnished place on Boulevard Magenta 20, in Paris' X'ième District. In the six days we were gone, practically everything was pilfered. We didn't know exactly who did it, but it must have been our beloved French neighbors, those anti-Semites. They took even stupid things like towels and bedspreads. There was nothing in the house. Somebody had come in and figured, *The Jewish people left and maybe they're not coming back.* More exactly, they undoubtedly said, *Sales Juifs!* which means, *Dirty Jews. They're out of here. We can break into their apartment and clean it out.* They never thought we'd come back alive.

My mother was pretty hysterical. She couldn't believe how this could happen. This was our home! You go away for a week and someone cleans out your whole place? It was devastating.

Somehow, we settled down. My mother had some money, so I guess she bought some towels, some blankets. The beds were still there. They didn't take out the major furniture or appliances, just whatever they could carry out. Of course, we still had no idea of the immensity of what was happening at the time.

When we went back to the farmhouse where we had left our Citroën, we found the car totally dismantled. The tires were gone, the radio was gone, everything gone. My mother's photograph albums, the only things she had thought so precious that she brought them with us, all gone. She had also taken the sterling silverware from her wedding. That, too, was gone. Every single thing was gone.

Our lives calmed down a little. It was business as usual in Paris, except that we were now under German occupation. The Germans were still trying to conquer England – which they never did – with the collaboration of the French. The armistice was brand new. The German's "master plan" had not yet been established. They did not officially begin making their so-called "round-ups" of the Jews until early the following year, 1941. The Germans were all over the place, living in Paris, but it wasn't so terrible.

There were curfews. Everything was rationed. Food was very restricted. Store shelves were empty. For some reason, I remember that there was an overabundance of bananas, especially later when we were smuggled out of the Occupied Zone. Food was extremely scarce, but you could eat all the bananas you wanted.

As a nine year old boy, this was a very scary time, very emotional. I remember a fleeting moment in which it occurred to me that I would never see my father again. That was a very traumatic thought. At that age, and with no disrespect for one's mother, one's father is the most important person to a boy. This feeling was very scary, disturbing, and emotional to me.

In Paris, we were no longer watching German planes strafing people on the ground. During our six or seven days on the road, while we were moving and when we were hiding in the woods, we watched them strafe. I knew they were shooting at soldiers, and while the civilian population at the time was more insulated, some were inevitably killed by accident. I didn't directly see anyone get his head blown off, but it had a disturbing effect nonetheless.

After that experience, I had a very bad feeling. We didn't yet think of German troops killing us – that had not yet begun to surface – but they projected an atmosphere of menace. It was a very strange, very upsetting feeling. At nine years old, being trapped with my mom made us both feel so helpless. At times, I felt that I could possibly kill a German soldier. Of course, for a child my age, that was a huge leap of the imagination.

It was the end of June. Although July is traditionally a holiday period in France, I don't recall going anywhere. We stayed in Paris.

At the end of August, I went back to my neighborhood public school, which was about two blocks away, when it reconvened. But I stopped going sometime in autumn. As a Jewish boy in a predominantly Christian neighborhood under Nazi control, it became uncomfortable to attend school. The kids beat up on me. After a couple of beatings, I came home one day and my ear was ripped and I was bleeding. My mother wouldn't let me go back to school after that. It was around October or November. My mother knew right then and there that we were heading for a rough time.

Meanwhile, one of my father's cousins, Frida Wattenberg, was in the French Free Underground (the Resistance), which was a whole movement dedicated to resisting the Occupation and saving people's lives. She came to my mother and said, "You had better start making plans because we got the word that they are starting to round up Jews."

They rounded up people in a very methodical way. They knew where you lived because they had registered you. They'd come to your apartment at 3:00 or 4:00 in the morning and knock on your door. *Get your clothes on. You're under arrest.*

"What's the reason?" you'd ask.

"Well, you have to speak to the police prefect." Or, "You'll find out down there."

These were French police who were in collaboration with the Germans. The Germans needed the French police to help. (Politically, after the war, France was in denial that they collaborated with the Nazis during the Occupation. Eventually, they did admit to their acts of collaboration.)

I never had the experience of being rounded up because we were forewarned by Frida.

My mother was scrambling around to see what she could do to escape. The northern half of France, which included Paris, was called the

French Occupied Zone because it was occupied by Germany. The southern half of France was unoccupied and known as the French Free Zone.
This was the agreement initially worked out with the Germans and Petain
(the Vichy regime). My mother had a mission, which was to get us out
of the Occupied Zone and into the Free Zone. From there, she planned
to get us into the United States to join my father. As far-fetched as it
sounds, that was her goal. She worked at it feverishly while I stayed with
my grandfather in his apartment in Paris. My mother was put in touch
with the Underground, probably through my cousin, Frida, and she was
busy getting documents and papers, figuring out a plan. I was not involved at all in the process – I was only nine years old.

I became very close with my grandfather during this period. He was
the only grandfather I had in France. With my father in New York and my
mother preoccupied with making plans, he was the one I depended on. He
was a wonderful guy. He was Orthodox. He wouldn't ride on Saturday.
He attended temple mornings and evenings. He would only walk to temple. He wore a *yamulke*. He laid *tefillin* every morning. He had a nice
beard. I was his only grandchild, so he showered me with a tremendous
amount of love. I remember small things, like the time in December or
January when it was cold out. I said to him, "Don't you have gloves?"

He said, "I have no gloves. But I have my hand. That's my glove."

Crazy thing to remember. Of course, I also remember when my
mother finally made her plans and there was a big so-called family meeting. My mother told my grandfather that we were planning to leave
within a day. She had made arrangements for him to come with us, but
he declined the offer.

"I'm not going anywhere," he said. "God will provide."

I was sad, but it wasn't traumatic. The Germans had perpetrated a
false sense of security by keeping their real plans so secret. As I said before,

Grandfather Isaac, 53 years old. Paris, 1940.

I honestly believe that unless you were in the Underground or the Re-sistance, none of the world's Jewish population was totally aware that the Germans had a master plan to kill everybody. We really did not know. It certainly didn't occur to me that we were on the cusp of being killed. Without knowing that, why would you have the fear? Especially since I was such a young guy. Of course, I'm sure my mother had her trepidation and her fears. She was single-minded in her determination to escape. That's why we are here. If it hadn't been for her stamina, her passion, and her courage, we would never have left, because what she did was very risky.

My mother's sister and her family, the ones who were in the car with us when we made our first escape attempt, refused to go with us this time to the Free Zone. They just didn't have the fear. My mother ag-gressively pursued plans to get us out of there, but her sister's thought was, *Where are we going? We'll go a little later.* Her sister had a baby girl and no family in America. She didn't have that passion to leave, just for the sake of escaping.

Of course, nobody knew that this guy Hitler was looking to kill all the Jews.

Smuggled Out, Staying Alive

My mother's plan was to get into the French Free Zone, then down to Marseilles, a shipping port in the south of France. From there, she hoped she could find a way to get to America.

I remember my mother trying to sell some of her assets so that we could have some funds, something of value to take with us. In Paris, there was a flourishing black market. My father had quite a nice business at the time, manufacturing men's clothing. So my mother liquidated a lot of the inventory that was left and converted all her French money into American dollars. In the black market, I remember they were selling American thousand dollar bills. Why do I remember this? Because my mother was trying to figure out how she was going to carry all that money. I'm assuming she had about $50,000. We are not talking about a bank account or credit card. We're talking pure cash. I remember my mother taking my socks – I always wore high socks. She took three or four thousand dollar bills, sewed them into the tops of the socks, and folded them over. She said, "You're going to carry X amount of money."

I had $10,000 worth of socks in thousand dollar bills! (One thousand dollar bills existed in United States currency.)

Somebody also must have advised her of the black market trade in diamonds that was prevalent at the time. You could take your money and convert it into diamonds. A diamond was the easiest commodity because of its small size. Let's say a diamond was worth four or five thousand dollars, it was better than carrying five thousand dollars in cash. I remember when we got to the United States, my mother had these little diamond chips, along with cash.

Without money, you were dead in the water. In the beginning of the war, if you had money at your disposal, it was a good bargaining chip. In late 1941, 1942, money became worthless because by then the Germans were treating Jews like dogs. Even if you had $50,000 in your pocket, they would just kill you and take your money. Life was meaningless. But in the beginning, they were like business people and would engage in cash transactions.

My mother made contact with professional smugglers (called *passeurs*), probably through my cousin in the Underground. We needed them to take us to the Free Zone. Although the line between the Occupied and Free Zones was an imaginary border, the Germans placed machine guns along that line. To cross the border would be like trying to escape from prison. Moreover, in the Occupied Zone, where we were, the Germans had implemented a system by which you needed a travel permit to go anywhere. We didn't have any travel permits, of course, so for us to travel from Paris to some unknown location would have been very difficult. So I believe we were driven about 300 miles from Paris to the spot where we were smuggled across the line. We only had a few clothes, because when you are running like that, it's not like you are going on holiday.

My mother paid the smugglers (*passeurs*) a certain amount of money, I'm not sure how much. I am sure the German soldiers guarding the border were in cahoots and that some of the money went to them. Many people who tried to cross that line of demarcation were killed, although we didn't realize it at the time. The Germans had orders, when they saw someone, to shoot on sight. For us to get through that frontier line can only mean that these German units were involved with the smugglers, most likely getting some of the cash.

I remember being smuggled across the border. It wasn't just my mother and I. We were with a group of about six or eight people, all being smuggled out. It was January or February of 1941, with snow and ice everywhere. We traveled only at night. There were no trucks, no nothing. We had to walk. We were in backwoods, rural farmlands. It might have been snowing, but I vividly remember being up to my waist in mud and water, trying to cross the marshlands. We were sneaking around. There were pre-arranged routes through little brooks and small swamps.

I remember one incident. We reached a brook and the smugglers put planks of wood down like a narrow bridge so that we could cross over the water. My mother said, "I can't do it. I'll fall in the water."

I said to her, "Don't worry." I was a bit of an athlete – I played soccer in Paris. I ran track. "Look, it's nothing," I said. I went right across.

"Don't go!" she said, but I went.

"Come," I said. I took her by the hand. The smuggler took her by the other hand and we went across. At that moment, she dropped her pocketbook in the brook, the pocketbook containing her money, all her papers, and the diamonds. It was a complete disaster. Fortunately, they retrieved it, which was a tremendous break. Talk about good luck. Without that pocketbook, we may have been in big trouble.

This whole experience was an adventure to me, a scary adventure.

I remember one time when I was absolutely frozen, blue in the face from shivering. There were no trucks or cars; we had no choice but to walk through the marshlands in the dead of winter. We had been walking for three or four hours when we arrived at a farmhouse at 10:00 or 11:00 at night. We were now in the Free Zone. The smugglers had made arrangements with farmers in both the Occupied and the Free Zones –

everybody was getting a piece of the action. On this night, the people were very kind. They saw I was freezing. There was no central heating in those days. They had a room set aside with blankets, but I was still shivering with cold. They warmed up bricks in their fireplace and put the bricks under the blankets. The bricks were not red hot. They were just warm. You laid the bricks on top of you, under the blanket, and that took the chill out. We slept well that night. It was wonderful getting out of all the mud, out of the freezing night.

We stayed in that farmhouse for a day or two. The rest of the group was now gone. It was just my mother and me. We were still involved with the smugglers. We had to go to Paux, France, which was maybe fifteen or twenty miles away. They took us to a hotel there.

Why did we need to go to Paux, a city that is near Toulouse? My father's brother, Morris, had been in the French army, but by 1940, he was no longer in the military. He was married and his wife was pregnant. Early in 1941, he was captured. The French police were collaborating with the Germans to round up Jews in the Free Zone. They put Morris and his wife, who was two or three months pregnant, in a "round-up" camp called Camp de Gurs. While there, he was listed three times for transport to the Final Solution, but he managed to dodge the convoy each time. We were able to correspond and he wrote, *Why don't you come to the camp?* So we went to Paux, which was near the camp, to be able to visit him in the Free Zone.

We went into what was called a "safe hotel" in Paux. Somebody must have been paying off the Germans, either the smugglers or the owner of the hotel, *they should leave us alone,* because there were already some Jews living there.

During the day we had a special permit. We could go into this camp, not knowing what we were doing. I used to go play with the kids there! Think about it! I actually went into a camp that ended up being a deportation camp, but at that time nobody knew it. I had to get a pass. It's like concentration camp, but in a concentration camp they wouldn't let you out. This one they wouldn't let you in! My uncle said, "I have my nephew. I want him to come in and play with the other kids."

I reflect upon the complete insanity of that situation, both that we went into a deportation camp to visit and that we were allowed out!

I would go in and play. I remember having a knife. I cut myself with it by accident and went to the clinic. I thought it was a camp! Like people here go to camp in the mountains? I went to deportation camp! Talk about a crazy world.

So that was our first stop after we were smuggled into the Free Zone. We stayed in Paux for about 10 days, recuperating from our travels thus far. Then one day, I remember it was in the middle of the night, the hotel owner came to my mother. My mother was a young gal of 30, and the owner said to her, "I'd like you to pack your things because tomorrow there's going to be a round-up. If you don't get out of here tonight, I think the Gestapo is going to take everyone away."

It was a very scary thing to be told this in the middle of the night, even if you're nine years old. We didn't have much to pack. What do you have with you when you are running for your life?

They were now rounding up Jews, even in the Free Zone. Even though the Germans had supposedly made an agreement with Petain, the President of Free France, and his Vichy government, to remain free, history has subsequently shown that they made another deal. The Germans told the French government that they had nothing against the French people, that the French could go about their lives in the Free Zone or the

Occupied Zone, for that matter. *But*, they said, *the Jews are causing trouble all over the world. Germany is in a Depression, the whole world is at war, and it is because of the Jews. Please help us to round up the Jews.*

In the Occupied Zone, it was most blatant. Starting in 1941, they were rounding up Jews, like my cousins, Jean and Jacqueline Bajczman. They put them in a huge arena, a big, closed-in stadium similar to Madison Square Garden in New York. I think it was called *Ile d'Hiver*, the Winter Garden. It could accommodate 30,000 or 40,000 people. They rounded up everyone – mothers, fathers, children – and put them under arrest. It was like a temporary waylay station while they were deciding what they were going to do. After all, they needed to have someplace to keep everyone while they were building the death camps. Like I said, if you are going to kill six million people, you have to have some kind of plan.

Initially, it wasn't so blatant in the Free Zone. But slowly, methodically, as 1941 progressed, the Germans in the Free Zone started to round up the Jews, with the collaboration of the French police. By 1942, Hitler no longer made any pretense of keeping his word at all. He said, *Forget the Free Zone. We're taking the whole country.* A lot of people had been escaping from the Occupied Zone into the Free Zone. He didn't like all these shenanigans. After the war, the big cry was, *Shame on France* and *Shame on the French police. Why did you collaborate in the killing and the deporting?* The truth was they didn't kill them in France. They rounded them up for deportation and sent them to the death camps in the East.

My Uncle Morris and his family – his wife had given birth to my Cousin Jack while in Camp Gurs – were part of a massive round-up in that camp in 1942. They were put on a train, where they were headed to Eastern Europe, meaning either Germany or Poland. While they were on the train, the French Underground sabotaged the railway and the train was derailed, somewhere near the Spanish border, late at night. They were being guarded by the French police, not the Germans. People just got off the train. The story goes that my uncle, his wife and their new-born baby got off the train and scampered into the farmlands. They went into hiding in the Pyrenees. They never went to Auschwitz.

My mother and I must have had some kind of permission to get on to the train in Toulouse, which we boarded and took to Marseilles. When we got to Marseilles, however, we couldn't walk out of the train station because they had a Gestapo agent and a French policeman at passport control. My mother began to cry hysterically. She wouldn't walk out of the station. She was trying to figure out what to do. I remember almost falling asleep on the bench in the station. It was like Grand Central Station, with thousands of people congregating and walking about. It was easy to get lost in the crowd, so my mother didn't stand out. Don't forget, the Germans were only targeting Jews. My mother was a blonde, blue-eyed, Aryan-looking girl. I was platinum blond with blue eyes. We certainly didn't look Jewish.

The German officer had to go urinate. My mother took a chance and walked right over to the French policeman. She said to him in French, "I'm here with my boy. I don't have any travel permits. You could probably destroy our lives. Have mercy."

The guy said, "Madame, I'm turning my head. Walk out with your son."

We walked out.

That was a big break. We didn't have travel permits. That's the way they would catch you, at passport control.

From there, we had an address of a certain hotel we could go to, another of the "safe hotels." This was all arranged through the Underground.

We arrived in Marseilles in February, 1941. We stayed there about five months. We began sending cablegrams to my father in New York to tell him we were alive. He thought we were dead. We had been completely out of contact – there was no way to communicate. There were no telephones, no communication whatsoever. We told him we were in Marseilles. We were going to register with the American Embassy. The United States was still in a neutral position with Germany. They had not yet entered the war.

I went to the beach in Marseilles. Why do I remember this? My mother had met some friends at the hotel. These friends stayed at the beach while my mother would go to the American Embassy to try to get a visa. I went to the beach with them and got sunburned, nearly third degree burns. So I remember that beach very well.

My mother went to the American Embassy every single day for about five months, from February to August, to apply for a visa. She was turned down every time. We didn't know it at the time, but Franklin D. Roosevelt and the American government were not very receptive to the Jews, even though they were sympathetic. The United States policy was not appropriate for the situation in Europe. America was coming out of the Depression and the government was concerned about people coming in and being on unemployment. So my mother couldn't get a visa because the quota had been completely filled.

My father was working to help us from the other side of the ocean, in New York. We must have gotten a cablegram in Marseilles from him when we were in the Free Zone. We later found out that he had been

My mother walking to the American Embassy trying to secure visas, Marseilles. July, 1941.

Visa that allowed my mother and myself safe passage from Marseilles to Spain to Lisbon and to set sail for America, 1941.

praying in temple for *Rosh Hashanah* in 1940 in the Bronx. By mere co-incidence, sitting next to him was Hyman Korn, who became a very critical guy in our lives. Mr. Korn was both a lawyer and Secretary to Congressman Buckley in the Bronx. He subsequently became a New York State Supreme Court Judge. As my father related the story to me, Hyman Korn saw him crying. He asked, "What's the matter, Leon?"

"Well, my son and my wife, they're in France. I don't know if I'll ever see them again. How can I get a visa for them?"

He helped get us the visa. It took seven months. Mr. Korn went to Washington with Congressman Buckley, who was supposedly Franklin Roosevelt's friend. They must have discussed our dilemma, which was that although my mother and my father had been living in France, they

Visa that allowed my mother and myself safe passage from Marseilles
to Spain to Lisbon and to set sail for America, end of August, 1941.

were officially Polish Jews. The United States quota system recognized only the natural place of birth, regardless of whether you were a nationalized citizen of another country. There was no room left in the United States for Polish Jews; the quota had already been met. But they figured out a loophole. I had been born in France. They figured, why can't we get a French visa wherein I, as a French citizen, am bringing over my mother? That's what they did. The visa says *Paul Wattenberg* and it states that I am the French citizen. With visa in hand, we were able to travel under safe passage of the American flag.

We left Marseilles by train, bound for Lisbon. It was a nerve-wracking trip because my mother was a nervous wreck. She was nervous because she knew little more about what was going on than I did. We were worried about how we were going to get past all the passport controls. It took us two weeks to get to Lisbon. When we arrived, my mother wrote a letter to my Uncle Morris and his family, who were still at Camp Gurs in France. My cousin, Jack Wattenberg, recently found the original handwritten letter in his father's file. The letter is dated August 19th, 1941. Reading it brings tears to my eyes. It rekindles all the poignancy of the events that took place and the family we left behind.

> My dear loved ones,
> We passed, surprisingly, a very agreeable voyage from Marseilles, via Spain, and have just arrived in Lisbon. I have sent you today several packages of cookies and chocolates and various things. I am writing you a few moments to say hello and if you see my sister and your father, tell them hello. Tell your father that our trip was better than expected and that we've arrived in Lisbon, thank God. I'm sending your brother a package for you. When we arrive in America, we will be happy to write you about our trip. I just thought I would

send you this card to make you aware of what's going on with us. I hope you receive this letter. I also am praying and hope that you will try to leave the camp you are in. The ship is leaving for America in one hour. I don't have a great deal of time left before we embark. I love you all. I kiss you with all my strength. I kiss you and wish you all well. Hope to see you someday.

— Rachel

My mother was very cautious with what she wrote, because she figured letters were being censored, which they were. She knew that her father-in-law, my grandfather Isaac, who had stayed behind, was very concerned about whether we would escape. According to the letter, the train ride was uneventful. The American visa gave us a window of opportunity, provided by a momentary loophole of which we were able to take advantage.

Voyage to America

We left Lisbon on August 19, 1941. We embarked on a small refugee ship. The trip itself was horrible. It was not one of these luxury boats from Carnival Lines. It was basically a freight ship where they took everything out – there were no cabins, no amenities, no nothing. They simply put down portable beds and blankets. There were about 400 people aboard, all sleeping in the hull of the ship. The seas were rough and I had a tendency to get sick. I was a total disaster. My mother took me to the captain, who was Portuguese. She begged him. "Look," she said. "I don't think he'll make the trip alive. He hasn't stopped throwing up since the day we got on the boat."

He took a liking to me. He said, "How can I stop you from throwing up?"

I said, "If there were some land, I could stand on it. I think I would stop throwing up."

Every captain has a tree on his boat. He had something like a palm tree. He was a strong guy. He lifted me up and put me on the earth of the tree!

He said, "Don't you feel better? I'll tell you what I'll do."

They let me sleep on the upper deck at night. Down below, everyone was throwing up. Little kids, nobody was sleeping. There were no separate toilets, only a common one. There was no privacy, but we managed to improvise. Generally speaking, though, it was a total disaster.

The scary part of this trip was when the captain told everyone to put on life preservers. There was a German U-boat in the area. I didn't know anything about U-boats and I certainly didn't know that we were subject to being sunk. I thought we were traveling safely on a Portuguese ship. I later learned that the Germans were using U-boats to sink American ships. Even though America was neutral, it was supplying England with armaments, shipping them across the Atlantic. The Germans decided that they had to stop that lifeline in order to have a better chance to conquer England.

I found out later that the German U-boat came alongside our boat and its sailors came aboard. The captain said, "Look, I just have women and children, a couple of older guys, all refugees. What do you want to do?"

The Germans gave us safe passage. They said, "You guys can go through."

So when you talk about life, I realize that everything in life is luck. This is the whole story of life. It's critical for everything. Whether it's your health, your business, marriage, family, friends or children, you need *mazel* (luck). Because when you think about it, we landed in New York on September 5th, 1941. We got off the boat the next day. On December 7th, a mere three months later, the Japanese attacked Pearl Harbor and America was in the war. We would never have been able to escape from Europe after that. We arrived during a window of opportunity that would last for only another 12 weeks.

Some of these things are very emotional. The truth of the matter is, when I arrived in the United States and started going to school, all these emotional disasters were buried deep in my memory. After all, I was only ten when we finally got out. I never really spoke about it. I almost didn't consider myself a Holocaust survivor after I learned what happened to the rest of our family. They really took the brunt of it: Auschwitz/Birkenau, the gas chambers, the crematoriums, the ovens. A most beautiful family, destroyed. I thought we were very lucky to escape. Although we were Holocaust survivors, I didn't really feel that I deserved to be called a Holocaust survivor.

So I realize that it comes back to *mazel* (luck): being at the right place at the right time. But it also came down to my mother's great courage. She had the desire to do what seemed impossible, to go beyond reality, as it were, and I guess I was her passion and driving force. Having a nine year old son probably motivated her to do everything she could to save herself and her child. In a case like this, your child is probably more important than yourself. She was also motivated by her husband being in America. She had a double motivation: to regain her husband and regain her life, our lives. She was an amazing woman. Along with luck, she was the reason we survived. ✱

My mother and me in our passport photo, Marseilles, France. August, 1941.

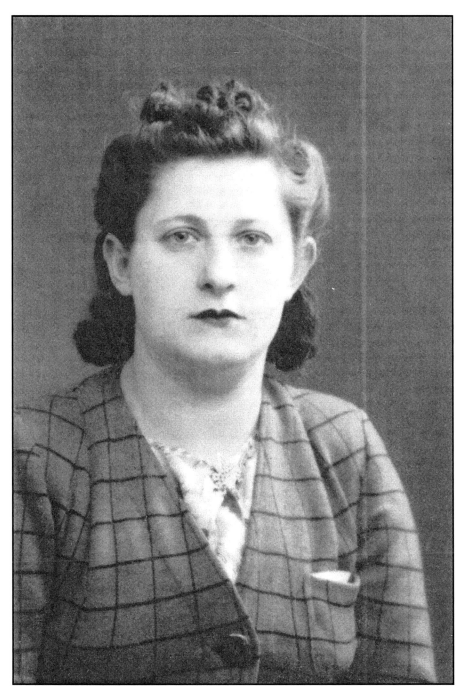

My mother's passport photo to leave France. Marseilles, May, 1941.

The Bronx, 1948.

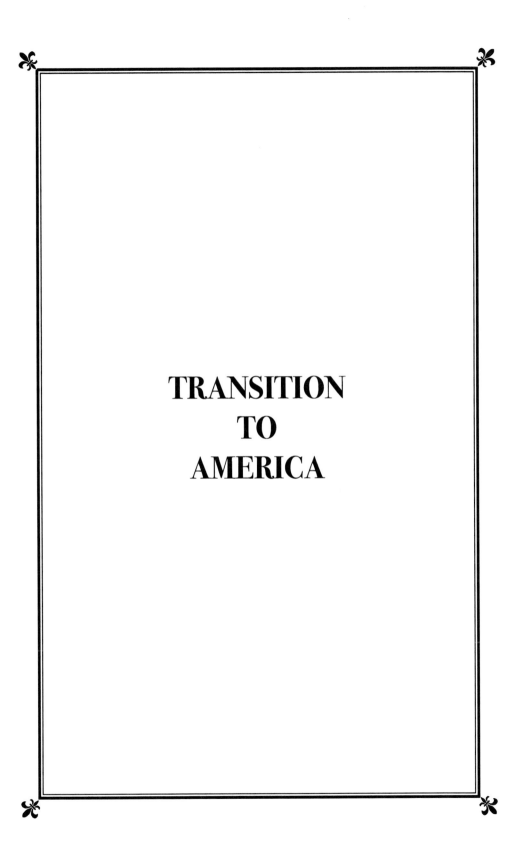

TRANSITION
TO
AMERICA

T he boat arrived in New York on September 5th, 1941, which happened to be Labor Day. We were not allowed to disembark because the Maritime Union wouldn't work on a holiday. I saw my father, from the ship's deck, for the first time in 25 months. He was standing on the dock. It was a very emotional moment. Subconsciously, I never thought I would see him again. It had been my dream during our entire time on the run, but realistically, I didn't believe it would happen. I collapsed into tears. We were so close, but still, I couldn't touch him. I couldn't hug him. We had to wait. He threw chewing gum at me! (As I read these words, I find myself flashing back, reminiscing about that moment, envisioning it again. Tears come to my eyes, just as they did then. It was such a happy, emotional moment, one I will never forget.) The distance from us to where he was standing was about 20 yards, maybe less. I was originally standing on deck, but in order to be on the same level as him, we had to go downstairs. We were allowed below. There were no cabins, no anything, down there – it was strictly a merchant ship. I ran down, just to be able to see him through the porthole.

Seeing him for the first time: that was the joyous moment of the trip.

The next day, we disembarked and it was a great reunion. We hugged. We kissed. A lot of tears all around. It was an emotional moment. The family made a big party. It was very exciting. Family was there whom I had never met – cousins, uncles. I didn't speak English, but I spoke French and Yiddish with my family. My mother and father spoke Polish, but I didn't.

My father's uncle on his mother's side (Pakula) was living in the East Bronx. He was one of those people who had immigrated in the 1920s. We didn't have a home, we didn't have an apartment, we didn't have anything, and he was nice enough to let us stay with him. We stayed there for about a week and then my father got an apartment at 2095 Creston Avenue, right off the Grand Concourse, also in the Bronx. We lived there for about six months, but we didn't really like it. It was a very tiny, one-bedroom apartment with a living room and a kitchen. There was another building on the corner of 182nd Street and the Grand Concourse. It was one of the few new buildings in the neighborhood, built right before the war. After about six months, we moved into that building and had a two-bedroom apartment.

My father was in the clothing manufacturing business. His firm in France was called *La Maison Léon*, which means *The House of Leon*. When he came to the United States, he called the company *Leon of Paris*. His company basically catered to the urban, male trade of the time, which was known as the zoot suit era. The zoot suit was a very *avant-garde* style of clothing, popular with young, fashionable Caucasian and African-American men.

My mother was a homemaker.

As far as religion was concerned, my mother's family were modern Jews. They were not Orthodox, although they had many children. My father came out of an ultra-Orthodox home, but he himself was a very modern Jew. He didn't wear a *yarmulke*. He observed *Shabbat* in his own way. During the rest of the week, he smoked three packs a day, but from sundown Friday night until sundown Saturday night, he didn't touch a cigarette. That was a huge sacrifice for such a heavy smoker! He would go to temple on *Rosh Hashanah*, *Yom Kippur*, *Passover*. We celebrated the holidays. Those were the main manifestations of Judaism in our house.

I was sent to school at Creston Junior High School, P.S. 79, which was right up the block. It was right in the beginning of the school year, September, 1941. At school, I was a celebrity of sorts. I didn't speak English and the teachers tried to be kind. They said, "Look, we have a French boy who just came from Europe."

I was immediately given the nickname *Frenchy*.

In my first semester, they put me in the fifth grade, according to my age. I was kind of a novelty, you might say. I didn't speak a word of English. I remember that the teacher, whose name was Mrs. Patrick, had the worst reputation. She was a real mean teacher from the 1940s who thought she was King Tut. Anyway, she requested volunteers. Each kid would get an hour or an hour and a half with me to teach me. They would walk around with me, point to a table and say *table*. Point to a chair and say *chair*. Lights, whatever. At first I sat there and didn't understand a word, but it was all kind of exciting. Having gone through everything we had gone through, to be in a classroom in America was an exciting thing.

I recall they pulled a little prank on me. This was maybe a couple of months after I arrived. They asked me if I could find some elbow grease. It was kind of a mean trick. Not really understanding what they meant, I went all over the school looking for elbow grease. Everybody went along with the gag!

I finished my first semester of fifth grade. I could hardly speak English. I got my report card. It said, *Not promoted. Unable to speak English.* I was pretty upset and depressed. Having just left the Holocaust and arriving in the United States, I had been all excited. Now I felt like a reject. I didn't realize it then, but looking back at it now, I was quite upset. I went home and showed the report card to my parents. Coming from the European theater, my parents still had a particular mentality, a feeling, about Judaism. *Keep a very low profile. Don't create waves because we have always been the underdog, just as today we are still the underdogs.*

My parents said, "All right, don't worry. You'll learn English. So you lost six months. Don't make a big deal."

So that was the end of that. In the meantime, there was a fellow in my class by the name of Shelly Fireman. He sat behind me. His report card also said, *Not promoted*. He and I were the only kids in the whole class who were not promoted. We became best friends. To this day, I am a partner in his restaurants, and he is one of the most successful restaurateurs in New York City. It was strictly serendipity that we were both left back. We've had a very special relationship and continue to bond 68 years later.

All told, I did learn English fairly quickly. I think I sort of meandered through the fifth and sixth grades. Emotionally, I was upset about being left back. It still bothered me. It wasn't until the seventh grade that I had a French teacher by the name of Mr. Bengis. My parents had encouraged me to take French because they were afraid I would lose all my French by the time I was in my later years. It turned out to be a very good suggestion because, to this day, I speak fluent French. Mr. Bengis was a very kind, very fine teacher. He recognized that even though I had been left back, I had a lot of creativity. He told me time and again, "You're really a good student and a very bright young man."

Mr. Bengis gave me a lot of wisdom and encouragement. From the time I met him, I turned around. I had been experiencing a feeling, not quite of depression, but of being somewhat rejected, substandard. I look back on it now and realize that I never felt that way after Mr. Bengis. He gave a big, encouraging boost to my confidence.

My brother, Gary, was born December 29, 1942. That was a very exciting moment for me. I had a brother! Because there was a difference of almost 12 years, which is huge for two kids, I was almost like a father-figure. This was especially true since my father was always working to build his career. But we had a tremendous bond even though we were so far apart in years. From the time he was born until he became a teenager, we were very close.

Life at home was good. To be with my dad was euphoria. Before the war, I had written to him from France that I dreamed about having a movie projector. After I arrived in New York, he bought me a wonderful eight-millimeter camera and projector. I'll never forget that.

At school, I really buckled down after Mr. Bengis gave me encouragement. I made friends, learned English, and I think I graduated top of my class from Creston Junior High. I was in the honor society, Arista. I was also very involved in athletics. I did the pentathalon, which is a contest consisting of five events: broad jumping; chinning; baskets (how many times you could shoot a basketball through the hoop in two minutes); the fifty-yard dash (I was the fastest fifty-yard dash kid in the class); and the broad jump. I came in third in the pentathalon. That was exciting. So I got a little recognition in athletics and academics. I had something like a 95 average.

I graduated from Creston Junior High School in the ninth grade. That was a very exciting moment. My parents were there. My brother was only about three or four years old. I remember going up on stage and receiving various awards for academics and sports.

I went on to DeWitt Clinton High School. I took the bus on the Grand Concourse to get there each day. This was the first time I did that, since the elementary school and the junior high were all in one building.

I think my high school sports career was unusual and pretty successful. In 1948, I played for DeWitt Clinton and our soccer team won the New York City championship. I played right forward. A fellow I played with, Ernie Elmreich, now lives near us in Florida, completely by coincidence. We met after not seeing each other for 50 years. It turns out he received a scholarship to play soccer at Brandeis University.

I continued my track career. I ran for DeWitt Clinton on the 880 relay. Specifically, I ran the 220 yard dash as a member of the 880 relay team, which meant that there were four people on the team and each passed the baton after 220 yards. We ran in every major event in the city. We were the number one champions in the Bronx. I remember that when we ran against Boys' High, we lost. They had a very strong urban team. But it was very exciting, nonetheless.

DeWitt Clinton High School track team, June, 1948. I'm third row, second from left.

I used to take my brother Gary to all the sporting events. I used to run in track meets in Madison Square Garden and Randall's Island, and he would always be there, even when he was five or six years old. It was very exciting for me. I think he liked it. Of course, he was so young that I had a problem: where was I going to leave him? Somehow we managed, because I definitely remember taking him to a few events. We had a special bond. We were close in those years.

I was also the pitcher for our softball team.

Coming from France, I knew nothing about American football, but I really wanted to play it, anyway. I tried out for the team. My track coach called the football coach and said, "Don't put Wattenberg on the team. He only weighs 135 lbs. The first time you guys tackle him, you'll break his legs."

As a consolation, I became towel boy for the team. I have pictures in the graduation yearbook where I'm sitting on the bench with a towel in my hand. My friend Shelly Fireman, who was the center of the team, which was a very successful team, I think they were city champs that year, was a very, very good football player.

My graduation from high school was also a very memorable occasion.

I was very social. Matter of fact, when this fellow Shelly and I were about 16, we printed up cards that read: *Shelly and Frenchy, the Greatest Lovers. Call anytime.* We distributed them. Nobody called!

We had some dates. I always had some girlfriend here or there, but I don't really recall anything serious.

Stowe, Vermont (before I broke my nose,)
1953.

Graduation from DeWitt Clinton High School,
January, 1949.

When I think back, it was kind of a tough era, growing up in the Bronx in those years. We lived in a very Jewish neighborhood, but drugs were rampant – marijuana, cocaine – a lot of crazy stuff was going on. To a lot of people, smoking marijuana was like having a cup of coffee. I credit sports for helping to keep me out of trouble. Of course, your mental attitude, as well as your parents' attitudes, are also important deterrents. But I think my heavy involvement in sports was a very strong influence. It even deterred me from smoking cigarettes. As a runner, I was told by many doctors that I had an excellent lung capacity and that any kind of smoking would diminish it. When I was 15 or 16, I did take a cigarette or two, but every time I inhaled, I started to cough. That turned me off to smoking cigarettes. I never smoked again.

I had a couple of friends who were heavily involved in drugs. They were the neighborhood coke addicts. I was pretty friendly with them, but I never really got too involved because they clearly had a substandard image of themselves, as reflected in their behavior. They passed away in their late thirties.

One of my friends was this fellow, Sam Moldovan, who, unfortunately, passed away very young. Heavy into the drug scene, he became addicted as a teenager. He, too, had escaped from the Holocaust. His mother and my mother had met and become friends when we were in Marseilles. Eventually, his mother got a visa to come to America. Our mothers reunited and rekindled their friendship. I probably became friendly with him because of our mothers' relationship. But he was one of these kids who, over and above marijuana and cocaine, also shot up heroin. It was a very sad thing. I kept in touch with him until his mid-thirties. He was always in trouble. He was in jail, always having problems. I would help him all the time with clothes and money. Every time he came out of jail, his mother would call and say, "Can't you help us?"

My father was in business. Comparatively speaking, we were a little better off than them.

Was I tempted? Did I ever smoke a joint? I might have. But I was never into it. And I can honestly look back and say, never cocaine, never heroin. Marijuana was never something that became a crutch. My friend Sammy couldn't go a day if he didn't take a shot of cocaine or heroin. He eventually killed himself with an overdose. That was a terrible story. I learned a moral lesson. A young guy destroyed his life. It was very sad.

Bar Mitzvah, 1944.

My mother, me and my father at my Bar Mitzvah, 1944.

From the time we arrived in the United States, New York was like a haven. Don't forget: we were coming out of hell. Life in the Bronx — how bad could it be? There was plenty of food. There was freedom of speech. There was a generally good reception. I had a Bar Mitzvah in 1944, for which my father made a nice, big party.

We had no idea what was happening to our family back in Poland. There was no communication. From 1940 until 1945, you didn't pick up *The New York Times* and go, "Look! They just killed another million Jews in Auschwitz."

There was no mail at all to Europe. We were kind of insulated because everything was so secretive.

Family portrait: My mother, me, my brother Gary (in front), and my father. Bronx, 1946.

By and large, I don't think the American Jewish community was aware of what was going on. There were sections of people who were more knowledgeable, like from the *B'nai B'rith*, or certain politicians, who got news. There was a trickling down of information that terrible things were happening in Europe, but it was all vague, shadowy, indefinite: *We aren't sure, we think it is.* If somebody came back with something to report, *The New York Times* would put a small article on the twelfth page. *They claimed they killed a lot of Jews. Who knows? Nothing's been verified. It's all hearsay.*

Yet there was a lot of legitimate information coming out through the Underground. Franklin Roosevelt was asked to drop bombs on the cattle cars bringing millions of people to Auschwitz. They begged him. All they wanted was American bombers to bomb and destroy some of these rails. This is exactly what happened to my uncle when members of the Underground exploded the rails so his train couldn't go to Eastern Europe, and the passengers escaped, including my uncle and his family. But Roosevelt refused and it never got done. The U.S. government's argument was, *How can we divert airplanes to use for this cause?* They were on dangerous missions to begin with, so it's true that there are two sides to this coin. But this was something huge that was really happening. ✳

Miami, 1955.

CAREER:
A SUCCESS STORY
(With a Few Bumps in the Road)

The Beginnings

After high school, I received a scholarship to the University of Wisconsin at Madison, but I didn't go there. My parents didn't like the idea of my traveling to Wisconsin. I also think it was a financial imposition on them. My father was having some trouble with the business, so I stayed nearby. I went to New York University (NYU).

I went to school full-time for about two or three years when, one day, my father called me into his office. He told me they were having financial difficulties with the business. We met with his accountant who told us that we weren't doing well as a company and maybe we should close up. "I don't know how you guys are going to continue," he said. "You haven't got that much capital left."

I guess in the spirit of trying to help my father, maybe give him a little courage, I said, "Don't worry. I'll go to NYU at night."

I was the new optimist in the company. "Don't worry," I insisted. "We are going to make it."

The plan was to change my schedule to work every day in the business for half a day, and go to school at night. My father said, "You'll work four hours a day. You'll go to school in the afternoon or the evening."

I did that, but I was tired all the time. I used to fall asleep in class. It became particularly difficult because the three or four hours a day that I was supposed to help out expanded to eight hours a day, from about 9:00 a.m. until 6:00 or 7:00 at night. It was a full day's work. Then I went off to class.

We went through a very hairy six months or a year. When I first came in, we had two cutters, two shipping clerks, two girls in the front office, and a couple of salesmen working alongside my father and me. My dad and I buckled down and cut our overhead. We laid off everyone except one shipping clerk, a guy named Al, and the bookkeeper. My father was a tailor and a cutter, meaning he cut the patterns. He took me in and taught me the business the hard way, from the bottom up. During the week, we would run the business. On Friday, Saturday and Sunday we would go in and cut the goods, which meant we had to cut the fabric from the patterns to send to contract factories to produce the clothing. This is how I learned to cut fabric. I also learned how to mark, meaning make the patterns. I also used to do the "joker tickets," which means you put size stickers on every garment. I also tied the bundles. I swept the floor. I cleaned up the whole place. It was a real apprenticeship.

It was a seven day work week. We worked around the clock, maybe 70 hours a week. We turned that business around and I learned it inside and out. As business improved, the family went on a trip to Europe without me in 1955. I was a little upset, but I understood that we all couldn't go. Someone had to stay home and mind the fort. My father was very appreciative. They went to Europe and had a good time. Upon his return, he said, "I didn't worry. I knew you were here. You helped watch the business."

We were located at One Union Square, at 14th Street, in Manhattan. Before we had to lay them off, we employed cutters, union guys who came in from the Amalgamated Union to lay in all the patterns. We had a cutting table, which was designed according to my father's exact specifications. He had figured out how to do the consumption, which means how much fabric you need to make a suit. I think it was maybe three yards and 20 inches. He built the table three yards and 20 inches times three, so it was 10 yards. I asked my dad, "How come you made such a short table?"

He said, "Well, anyone comes in to work here, if they need a longer table, they can't work here, because it means they are going to use too much fabric."

The table provided a built-in means of consumption control.

I said, "What happens if you do bigger sizes?"

He showed me a little extension at the end of the table, a leaf, that he could open up.

That is how I learned the business. Watching, asking questions, doing. My father took me around to the factories. He took me to the fabric market. I had to learn textiles. At that particular time, the late 1940s, early 1950s, there was a big craze for jitterbug zoot suits. Those were suits with broad shoulders and longer jackets. We made them with Hollywood rise pants, which were pants with a one-piece waistband, 26 inch knees and a 15 inch bottom. We'd sell the suit with a chain. These suits were geared towards a special market that catered to young white and black men who were, let's call it, cool guys. Those were the clothes they liked.

There was another trend happening at that time, maybe a couple of years later. My friends at NYU didn't want to wear zoot suits. It wasn't the right look. We started to make a suit called "Jivey Ivy," which boasted a natural shoulder, no pleats, a more contemporary styling, much like Ralph Lauren is doing today. It was a more updated look. The Ivy look was something that was being worn at University of Pennsylvania, Yale, Harvard, Dartmouth – all the Ivy League schools. Fast on the heels of the zoot suit, it was a little younger in feeling.

At the particular time, the Who's Who of our industry were all located on Fifth Avenue between 14th Street and 23rd Street. We, however, were on Union Square. We dreamed of being on Fifth Avenue. After we turned the business around, which took probably two years, we moved. We relocated to 97 Fifth Avenue, on the corner of 17th Street. We had the second floor. The business really started to move a little bit. We were making both "Jivey Ivy" and jitterbug suits. Matter of fact, my father had a sign on Union Square before we moved. It said, *Leon of Paris, Home of the Jitterbug Suit, Specialist in Peg Pants*. "Peg" meant that the bottom of the pants was very tapered. If you had a shoe on, you couldn't get your foot through.

We moved to 97 Fifth Avenue and started doing really well. Then a real bummer took place. I was out of town, traveling on business, which I sometimes did for a week here or there. My mother called me and said, "Please come home right away."

My father was ill. On December 10th, 1959, we met with the hematologist. He told us that my father had acute leukemia and had maybe four weeks to live. This was a complete shock. Today, with advanced medicines, he may have had the opportunity to go into remission, but in those days, his type of leukemia was always fatal. He never knew how sick he really was. The thinking in those days was, *Don't say anything to him.* Who wants to tell someone, *You've got four weeks to live?* Even though we were told, for all practical purposes, he never knew it himself.

On January 16th, 1960, he passed away. He was 51 years old. I was a total basket case. I was 28 years old. For eight years, he and I had been together all day, every day. Not only did we work together, but I lived at home. We were together 24 hours a day, seven days a week. His death was a huge emotional set-back for me.

My father died without a will, *in testate*. Legally, when a business owner dies *in testate*, the business automatically gets left to the spouse or the surviving siblings, I don't remember. In any case, the end result was that I was left with the business. My brother was only 17 years old, a student at DeWitt Clinton High School, so he was not involved. My mother said she would help me get back on my feet. My father had a life insurance policy which, unfortunately, he had borrowed against. When we went to cash it in, we got all of $5000. The whole policy was maybe for $20,000, but $15,000 went to the bank. There really wasn't much money left.

My mother and father, c. 1955.

I was completely devastated. I was suddenly shouldering a huge amount of responsibility. As I said, my brother was still in public school. There was nobody but me to run the entire manufacturing concern. Frankly, I was so distraught that I didn't know if I even wanted to continue in the business.

I went into mourning for a couple of months. I didn't feel like going to work. I was very depressed and felt very alone. But I finally decided to regroup and try to keep this business afloat. I was very fortunate. While we didn't have much money, we did have a solid foundation. I had knowledge and experience with all aspects of the business – sales, design, all the ingredients – after having worked with my father for those years. Plus we had the business itself, which was up and running, and a solid customer base. I worked very hard and was able to put it back on its feet and make it work.

These things are part of life.

My mother came in to help me. She knew about production, cutting, things like that. We worked together while my brother was in high school. Within two years, rather than going to college, he came to me and said he had met a girl and was getting married. I said, "Aren't you going to college?"

He said, "No. Can I help you in the business?"

He married Myrna and they had four children: Les, Jill, Gregg, and Eric.

I took him in and made him a partner. I gave him a third of the company. My mother kept a third, and I had the other third. The business evolved.

Building the Business

Although I considered dissolving the business after my father died, I ultimately decided not to. I think a couple of things happened. At that time, there was a company called *Ripley Howard Clothes*. My wife's maiden name was Newman. The owner of *Ripley* was a man by the name of Sam Newman, although no relation to my wife. Sam Newman's son-in-law was Howard Moss. Newman and Moss were manufacturers. They manufactured their own goods. At that time, I had a very creative mind. I had already established a reputation for making some very unusual, advanced fashions for men, very *avant-garde*.

I went to see Sam Newman. He spoke with a little Jewish accent. He said, "Why do I need you? Why do I need you?"

He had a big plant in Brooklyn. He was one of the largest producers in the United States at the time.

He said, "I make my own goods. You can't compete with me. I buy the fabric. I make the garment. What are you going to offer me?"

I said, "Well, I think I could offer you something that would bring a new customer into the store."

He decided to take a chance. He gave me an order for maybe 8,000 or 10,000 suits. At the time, it cost about $10 to make a suit, with fabric costing about $3 a yard. Nineteen dollars times 10,000 suits, it must have been $190,000 worth of suits he ordered. This was a huge order in those days, especially for me in a small company.

I then went to the textile mill, Bachman Textiles. The credit manager turned me down. He said, "We can't give you $100,000 credit. Your net worth is only $100,000. How can we give you $100,000 credit?"

I asked to see Lou Bachman, the president of the company. I brought the orders in to show him. I said, "Look, I've got all these goods sold to Ripley." He knew they were a good customer.

"You've got to trust me," I said. "How much would you want to give me? Whatever it is, you've got to trust me."

Lou Bachman somehow had confidence in me and it was a big breakthrough. He gave me credit beyond what we were entitled to so that we could get the material and produce the garments. I started doing a lot of production and we began to make a profit. That was the beginning.

In April, 1960, three months after my father died, we moved the business to a new place, 126 Fifth Avenue. We had three floors. One floor was a warehouse, one floor was an office, and one floor was the cutting area. It was very difficult to work on three floors, but we were there for about seven years.

In 1968, we moved to 23rd Street. That was another big move. We took one floor in a building with Gramercy Park Clothes and Petrocelli. Those were the famous brands of the day. That floor was about 45,000 square feet. We had cutting rooms, our office, our warehouse, and our design room, with many employees, all on one floor.

We kept that place and in 1973, we also opened up a showroom at 1290 Sixth Avenue. The whole men's wear industry had moved to 1290, which was on the corner of 51st Street and Sixth Avenue.

Adolfo

At that time, my wife, Linda, was an Adolfo customer. He was a *couturier* with a studio on 57th Street. Linda used to go up there to buy her clothes. She'd meet Jacqueline Kennedy, Nancy Reagan, Betsy Bloomingdale, all the famous people. Adolfo had very good credentials. There

Mr. Adolfo and me, c. 1989.

was an Adolfo ladies' boutique in every Saks Fifth Avenue store and in every Neiman Marcus store. So that gave a very good cachet. Adolfo was the Chanel of the early seventies. He studied with Balenciaga in Europe in the early fifties. He had a very good flare. Let's call it the Adolfo look. It was synonymous with Chanel and it was a very successful concept at Saks and Neiman Marcus.

I first met Adolfo when I went to his studio with my wife to shop. I forget whether we had coffee or lunch, but we started talking. I had always been seeking to produce the perfect suit, but I didn't really think outside the box. I broached the idea of him giving us a license for menswear. He was reluctant to do it. I said, "A men's line, you don't make men's, so it can't conflict."

He was very protective of his brand. He didn't want anything to hurt it.

I said, "Look, we're making men's wear. You don't do that. Men's suits, sports coats, overcoats, slacks, sweaters."

Initially, Adolfo didn't want to license his name. He wanted to control everything because he was making very high-priced clothes. His average couture suit was between $2500 and $3500. In today's thinking, that's very inexpensive. But in those days, it was very high-class stuff. As a matter of fact, today, a little of the Adolfo look is in both St. John and Chanel.

Finally, we made a deal. This was a pivotal moment in my business life. We didn't initially have a joint venture. I just took a license from him. Over time, as we got to know each other, we became equal associates. Eventually, as business affiliates, we handled all his licensing on an exclusive basis. This gave our company a designer handle and a designer brand, which was tremendously helpful in the growth of the business.

We designed the line together. My company had been doing men's apparel since 1931. We were certainly very professional in this area. But Adolfo was always involved, making sure that the line had a certain look. He wanted to be sure he was comfortable with it. We agreed to this as a courtesy to him, but we certainly liked his input because he's a talented guy.

We launched the Adolfo line in 1974. Launching Adolfo was a special moment in my life. We did a tremendous amount of public relations and advertising in preparation for the launch. For instance, Percy Sutton, who was the Borough president of Manhattan, declared *Paul Wattenberg-Adolfo Day*. We also made a deal with the Broadway show, *The Wiz*, and threw a wine and cheese party at the Minsky Theater that was more like an extravaganza. We invited 1500 people from all over the United States who worked within the industry. It was on a Monday night when the theater was closed, and we re-opened it and staged a fashion show with the whole cast. We had an amazing turnout. I saw a retailer just the other day who said he remembers that night vividly, it was such an exciting evening. Fifteen hundred people at a party. That's a lot of people!

Nancy Reagan was Adolfo's most famous customer. When Ronald Reagan was elected President the first time, Adolfo created the little red dress that Nancy wore to the inauguration. Her image was on television and flashed throughout the entire world. Nancy Reagan wearing Adolfo's little red dress gave us a lot of notoriety. Today, that red dress is on display at the Smithsonian Institute in Washington, D.C., a piece of fashion history for all of posterity.

In the mid-sixties through the mid-seventies, Adolfo would do trunk shows, meaning he would make personal appearances at the stores that sold his clothing. If Saks had a store in Beverly Hills or Boston, he would make a personal appearance. That was a big plus. Over a period of years, Adolfo developed a large personal following throughout the United States.

I had plenty of trepidation before I joined up with Adolfo, because there were minimum guarantees, which were a lot of money at the time. What finally convinced me to do it is an interesting story. While I was negotiating with Mr. Adolfo, I happened to have a particular customer in San Francisco. This guy had about seven or eight stores on the west coast. Before Adolfo, we had a private label called *John Hampton*. This customer used to buy a couple of thousand of our *John Hampton* garments a season. All of a sudden, I noticed the number of garments he ordered from us was beginning to decline. From 3,000 one season it dropped to 1,500, and then to 1,000. I was pretty friendly with him. I said, "What's going on?"

He said, "Well, I just took in Pierre Cardin. If you could get me a designer label, I would certainly buy a lot of goods from you."

Right on the spot, I said, "Look, you see this whole line?" I had the contract from Adolfo, but I hadn't signed it yet. "How about I give you this garment? It's going to cost you $40 more a suit. I have to pay royalties and we made it with a much better lining, better fabrics, better everything." It was a much higher class garment.

He said, "No problem. I'll give you 4000 units if you can get me the Adolfo label."

I shook his hand and did not tell him that I didn't yet have the contract.

The next week I went up to Saks Fifth Avenue and spoke to the president. I told him I would like to give him the launch in the United States. Even though I had a tentative order from the guy on the west coast, I figured he would wait six months because I really wanted to give the launch to Saks Fifth Avenue, which was a more prestigious store. I don't remember if I went up with Mr. Adolfo, but Saks knew we were associated. They gave us the launch, but they wanted it to be exclusive. I couldn't sell to anybody else. So I gave them the exclusive launch for the first six months or a year.

We did all the public relations and advertising. We had a whole marketing plan. We were on billboards in every important airport in America. When you drove to J. F. Kennedy International, you saw an Adolfo billboard. You went on the Long Island Expressway to the Queens Midtown Tunnel, on the right side, we had billboards. We launched at every airport in Los Angeles, San Francisco, Chicago, Miami, Boston, New York, Philadelphia, Detroit. Every time you got off the plane, you would see the name Adolfo. As a matter of fact, I had a sign, which we made specially, right across the street from Bloomingdale's in New York, even though we couldn't sell them. Right at the corner of 61st, staring directly into their store. Two years later, when we wanted to sell them, they took in the line.

We sold at all the most prestigious stores in America. We sold coast to coast at upscale stores of the highest caliber and class.

We also did plenty of television. We were on the *Merv Griffin Show* with Bob Hope, Frank Sinatra, Red Buttons, Billy Daniels. Mr. Adolfo was interviewed. I was interviewed. We'd bring them to the showroom. Bill Beutel of *Good Morning, America* would come in and interview Mr. Adolfo with the camera there. *Ladies and Gentlemen, Mr. Adolfo with Paul Wattenberg, launching their Adolfo men's wear collection.* We had a special showroom. The business was growing. It's still in existence today.

From the time we started with Adolfo, we had a lot of fashion shows. We used to run a fashion show at the Metropolitan Club on 62nd Street. We also had shows in Las Vegas and Los Angeles. We had breakfast showings for the press. We really did a lot of unusual things. These events gave us a lot of notoriety, which was excellent for public relations, a very important aspect of our business. Andy Warhol used to come to all our shows. To me, he wasn't such a big deal. I wasn't that sophisticated in the arts. I didn't realize that here was a great artist and an icon of the twentieth century. He was Mr. Adolfo's good friend.

Of course, I was very involved with all the sales, all the salesmen. I used to travel the whole width and breadth of the country for work: networking and sales.

We then developed an expanded licensing business. When the mens' line had proven to be successful for three or four years, we made a deal with Adolfo to license other products, such as luggage, home goods, colognes, shoes, umbrellas, ladies' suits and dresses, sweaters, outerwear, hats, makeup and cosmetics, panty hose, intimate apparel. We did furs. The license business exists to this day. We do all the licensing. That is a very big plus. I think I was a little bit ahead of my time. Today, everybody is jumping into the fray. Licensing is major business. At that time, it wasn't so common.

Me and Lee in Adolfo showroom on my 73rd birthday, 2004.

Without question, being involved with Adolfo was a major blessing. Not only was it a good business decision, but on a personal level, our meetings, dinners, and get-togethers have been a source of great joy for me. Adolfo is a very fine gentleman, very private, extremely kind, and he is always there when needed.

Ups and Downs

Over the years, there have been ups and downs. In the 1980s, there was a period of exorbitant interest rates, which went up as high as 21%. The cost of doing business was very tough. There are always ups and downs. Nothing goes in a straight line.

I hired a licensing director in 1979 who helped to run my license business. He was two years younger than me. His name was Neil Tessler. I had a meeting with him one Tuesday in 2006 in my office. We spoke about all kinds of things. He walked out of my office, went to 40th and Broadway, collapsed in the street and died. It was very sad. Throughout the years, Neil was a good friend with a great flair for fashion. He was a great talent in our industry.

Concorde

Our business was called *Leon of Paris* until 1995. It was a very big company with a large number of employees. Then we ran into some problems. We were producing our goods domestically, as we had always done. But we were in a changing industry. There had begun to be a heavy influx of imports from all over the world. I could see that production of goods in American factories was becoming increasingly difficult because of high labor costs. I really felt in my heart that the future would be to manufacture our goods overseas. It was a very soul-searching decision. We had been manufacturing our own goods in the U.S. for 54 years, ever since my father started it up in 1941. But as a highly unionized American company, we now faced huge obstacles trying to go overseas. The unions were fighting free trade.

Free trade was inevitable, however. It became a very important goal for us to get into the business of importing our goods. It was the wave of the future. Today, virtually 100% of all men's apparel is manufactured outside of this country. The same is true of textile production: it is all produced overseas.

When I went into the business in 1950, there must have been 200 men's clothing manufacturers in the United States. Now, I think there are four. The entire American apparel business, with the exception of a couple of large companies, has outsourced its production overseas, meaning that the goods are manufactured in foreign countries. It's a survival strategy. In a global free trade market, you have to compete on an international scale. The auto industry is currently going through a challenging era and must adjust or else it, too, will have problems surviving.

By the 1990s, domestic clothing manufacturers were being overwhelmed by international imports and were not able to compete. As imports flooded this country, our company fortunately phased out domestic operations and transferred all production to overseas facilities. My son Lee runs the company, which is now a good import business called Concorde, with products manufactured in Europe and Asia. Adolfo is still the brand name. Lee is doing a great job, with fantastic success, beyond all our expectations.

Business Highlights

Meeting and affiliating with Adolfo was certainly a very special part of my business life. He heightened our business cachet and gave it a tremendous boost in prestige and class. He himself is a very fine gentleman, very understated, with a lot of class. He's really an icon from that era. What I say, "that era," I mean myself. He is basically from the era of Yves St. Laurent, Pierre Cardin, Halston, Perry Ellis, Giorgio St. Angelo, just to name a few. He is one of the few icons of that era who is alive and still functioning very well and has a very, very nice way about him. He is very well-recognized by the press and with the great celebrities but, speaking to him, you would never even know that these were his clients because of his understated nature and his shy way. He never flaunts anything. He's very conservative. He's very elegant and a very classy gentleman. He and I have been together now since 1975. That's a span of 35 years. It's been a very, very good, smooth relationship.

Other special events are when we launched Adolfo with many, many fashion shows at the Metropolitan Club and the fashion show at the Minsky Theater I spoke about earlier with the entire cast of the musical *Wiz*, put on for 1500 people. It was quite an unusual evening.

We also had the launch of a line by André Courrèges, a French designer and couturier. We hooked up with the French Embassy on Fifth Avenue and they let us use the entire place. We had a fashion show and the Who's Who from all over America attended, from Bert Tansky, who today is the CEO of Neiman Marcus, to the various CEOs of the various companies, Bloomingdale's, etc. I think that was very special.

Another very special event was when I was made *Man of the Year* by the Association of New York Retailers in 1977. It was a nice accolade. I made a speech that night and my mother was still alive. It was a very unusual night. The Who's Who of the retail business was there. I felt it was an expression of how lucky I was to be in America, thinking of how at that time we had already launched Adolfo and we were having very, very good business and notoriety, and it was only in a country like America where you could start from the bottom and build yourself up. It was a very special evening.

I also think a very unusual evening was when Sy Syms, from Syms, suggested that I be nominated to receive the "Lion of Judah Award" in recognition of service to Israel. The cocktail reception and ceremony was held on January 21, 1987 at the Plaza Hotel in New York City to help to raise funds for Israeli bonds. It was a very special evening which I think is best described in a newspaper write-up in the *New York Post* we received at the time:

BULLISH ON BOMBS:

Sy Syms threatened to read one of his commercials if the assembled guests in the Crystal Room of New York's Plaza Hotel didn't seat themselves pronto. That seemed to do the trick. As the room full of 'educated consumers' eventually quieted down after some preceremony imbibing and scoffing down of hôrs' d'oeuvres, Syms spoke of his good friend, Paul Wattenberg, the honoree of the evening. As the president and chief executive officer of Adolfo/Leon of Paris looked on, Syms – in a flourish of fundraising acumen – raised $700,000 in Wattenberg's name for State of Israel bonds. And putting his money where his mouth is, the Forbes 400 inductee didn't have to dig too deep in his pockets – undoubtedly just scraping the surface – to match that amount, bringing the grand total pledged to $1.4 million.

Those investing in the bonds, which help Israel become economically independent through the development of high-tech industries and economic development projects such as the construction of dams and apartment houses were industry stalwarts all, including Harvey Weinstein, Jerome Schottenstein, Stanley Blacker, David Feld, Bernard Feinberg and others too flush to mention.

Clutching the plaque which cites his leadership and active participation in the Israel bond program, Wattenberg recalled his youth as a persecuted Jew smuggled out of German-occupied France as a nine-year-old. Wattenberg said he learned early on that independence and the right to live in a free state are precursors to freedom.

It was a very memorable evening and I was happy that I was able to help Israel and raise that kind of money in a short amount of time. I was honored to be their nominee. Sy is a close friend of mine, by the way. My wife, Linda, and I have become good friends with him and his wife, Lynne.

I've also had the honor to be written up in many of the trade papers, and to have achieved a certain recognition within the industry by many peers whom, I think, respect my fashion direction and my color sense.

Another very unusual event in my life began when Frank Sinatra walked into a store in Vegas called Cousins. He bought half a dozen Adolfo tuxedos. While in that store, he was with a friend by the name of Dennis Stein. Dennis was someone I knew all my life. He took Frank Sinatra to the side. He said, "Why do you buy retail? Let me call my friend Paul. He does all the Adolfo tuxedos. I'll get them for you from the factory."

Sinatra got on the phone and called my secretary, Andrea. She said, "Who's calling?" and he said, "Frank Sinatra." True story. She hung up on him! Three times. She figured it's a hoax.

Eventually, Dennis Stein got on the phone and said, "Let me talk to Paul. Please don't hang up. I'm with Frank Sinatra. We want to come up to your warehouse and get a lot of clothes. Frank likes your tuxedos. They're the best tuxedos he's ever worn."

At that time, I got very friendly with Frank Sinatra. I spent about six months romancing him and trying to work on a concept, a Frank Sinatra collection. Unfortunately, it never came to pass, but it was kind of a euphoric moment in my life, because he certainly is an icon. I didn't really capitalize on it, although I have a picture of Frank and myself in my office, which is my claim to fame as far as Frank Sinatra goes.

I do have another special memory that indirectly involves Sinatra. A year or two ago, I had lunch with the senior executive vice-president of JCPenney, Lana Cain. She was very funny. She's very successful, third in command of a twenty-four billion dollar company. A big success. We got very friendly. She heard that I sing at these parties. She also likes to sing.

We were having a men's apparel show in Las Vegas in February, 2007. A dinner was going to be held at the S&W Steakhouse at the Wynn Hotel. I suggested to her that we sing together. I said, "I'll send you the lyrics to *My Way*. You and I are going to get up in the middle of the restaurant, when all our peers are there, we're going to sing *My Way*."

She said, "You've got a deal."

We did it. It was funny. It's on video.

It was one of the most enjoyable evenings of my entire career. Having organized a bit of background music, I gave everyone at the table the lyrics to *My Way*. At the table was Steve Lossing, the Vice-President and DMM of JCPenney for menswear. It was Steve who introduced me to Lana Cain and who has been a friend ever since. My wife Linda, my son Lee, and Orlando Velez were all there. On the spur of the moment, when we finished singing Frank Sinatra's *My Way*, the background music per-

Frank Sinatra's birthday party. Me on left, Sinatra on right. New York City, 1985.

son suggested we sing *Strangers in the Night* and gave us the lyrics. It was a memorable, unusual, special evening of friendship, food and bonding.

Reflections on Career

I have always had a very special feeling for fashion. I love the creativity, the interesting styling. Putting the collections together was always an exciting challenge. My son has eased into it very well. He has a way of doing things that are similar to me, but he also does his own thing. He's not as much a workaholic as I am. He spends much more time with his kids and family. Bravo! I applaud that. He has his values in the right place.

I was, I am, a workaholic. It was about ambition, passion for the business, a zest for fashion. I also think that I was in part shaped by my humble background. In Paris, I watched my dad and my mother work 14, maybe 15 hours a day making custom-tailored suits, just to earn a living. We lived in a cold-water flat when we came to New York. I watched their battle to get out of that ghetto-type of atmosphere. These memories have remained with me. They are always in the back of my mind. Maybe they created a fear. I don't know if that's the right word. My dad built everything with his own hands. He didn't inherit any money. I think that knowledge, that memory, trickles down into your mind, becomes a part of your psychology. You always have the thought in the back of your mind that you don't want to return to that state of being, that *déjà vu*.

The lust for life, the zest for life, the feeling for having good health, having a family, living the good life, is also important. You need to be somewhat of a success to be able to reap the enjoyment of what you have earned. I was kind of driven by the need to live a life filled with the finer things and to provide for my family. At heart, I always feel poor. You may call it workaholic, it may even be an emotional disturbance. I always worry for tomorrow, more so than I probably have to. Some people are very hunky-jolly, and if they have a dollar in their pockets, they are just as happy as if they had ten million dollars. Some people are not. I'm one of those who fall into the "not" category. I could have ten million and I'm still concerned about being poor. No matter how confident I am, in the back of my mind, I'm always concerned about tomorrow.

I am a risk-taker. I think that if you want to go along with the mainstream, you will never have the opportunity for a *raison d'être*, meaning a reason for existing, a reason for being. You have to have a vision, a reason why you believe in a certain fashion, or a reason for being in business. You need to have a definitive point of view and a very definitive philosophy, believe in it, and take a chance on it. Of course, when you take chances, you're not going to bat 100%. But at least it's better to make a leap of faith – like the old saying goes, *It's better to have loved and lost than never to have loved.* If you took no risks, you'd never be able to experience the range of life's possibilities. You have to believe in yourself.

There are several ways to design. All design comes about from an inspiration, or a piece of art, or maybe from an antique store with antique clothing that was done 50 years ago. In reality, everything repeats itself, with some variations. Designing is an interpretation of something you envision as a possibility, something that you've done before and reinterpreted, or something that's been done by someone else and you reinterpret.

You have to be a student of fashion. From the time you design something until it is sold in stores, there is a significant passage of time. You have to have the eye and the nose to predict fashion, to visualize what is going to sell a year later. This also applies to the idea of color. One needs to predict the colors that will be in fashion a year or so down the line.

I think that besides being a student of fashion and color, you also have to have a gut feeling, an instinct. If you bat 85% or 90% of the time correctly, you are doing pretty well. In essence, you are predicting the future. You need to trust your instincts and be willing to take a leap of faith.

I was, and am, that type of student. I've always enjoyed fashion. I love color. As a matter of fact, when I first got married, I tried to paint. But fashion is something you have to have a passion for. You have to believe in it. You have to take risks, be different. I once saw a sketch that showed about 50 heads. Everybody was in the same line, but one person was heads above the crowd. The only way he was able to get heads above the crowd was to stick his neck out. While all the other heads were in a line, his neck was stretched out, above all the rest.

You must be creative. Sometimes creativity can transcend realism, go beyond envisioning what is merely sellable. That's the fantasy of fashion. Victoria's Secret had a show on television the other night that was all fantasy undergarments, using the most beautiful women in the world. All fantasy.

We used to do fashion shows and fantasy was an important part of the image. We had both male and female models because, while we were a men's line, the women were the fantasy part. Let's say you made a tuxedo, you'd have the girl wearing an evening dress. If the two of them walked down the runway with music in the background, it was more dramatic. It's theatrics. All these fashion shows are theatrics, like putting on a Broadway show. A lot of stuff is shown that most people won't wear, but it gets the *oohs* and the *aahs*. And if you look behind the scenes at Victoria's Secret or any of these other fashion shows, the designers are backstage. They want to make sure the model has the right hairdo, the right lipstick, or the guy is dressed correctly. It all circles around sex. Sexuality becomes a part of the fashion. That is the message, the fantasy, that you are selling. However, at all times, the clothes need to be elegant and sellable.

You have to be a good businessman. Practicality is important, too. You have to make a line of clothing that the average woman who walks into the store will be able to wear. You have to have a quality product. Specifications, dimensions, the fit of the garment – these are all essential elements. Ultimately one has to mix fantasy with reality, practicality with what is called "runway pieces." The fantasy is a very important part of creating the image you want to project to sell your line of clothes. But ultimately, whether it's men's or women's, the product has to be made right. If it is, it has a very good chance to be successful.

My father had a very good sense of fashion. He developed his niche in the 1940s and 1950s with the jitterbug suits and zoot suits, specializing in peg pants. His niche was popular in his era, but then things changed. You have to change with the times.

Visualize a ferris wheel. A ferris wheel interpreted into fashion means this: on the ferris wheel, there are different seats. Let's say that each seat represents all the fashions from a certain era. With all seats combined, the ferris wheel contains every imaginable fashion that has ever existed. The ferris wheel is turning. My challenge is to pick the right fashion off the right seat at just the right moment. That takes perception and acumen.

Let's talk about women's wear. The miniskirt, which was big in the 1960s, will come back again. But you have to know when to take it off the ferris wheel and put it back into the production line. Every time there's a new generation, something old has the potential to come back into play.

Right now we are selling a very hip, skinny, double-breasted suit. Double-breasted suits have been around for the last 100 years. A few years ago they didn't sell, but now the timing is right, so double-breasted suits have come back into the picture. Another example are vests, three-piece suits. For a while now, vested suits haven't sold. Now, all of a sudden, we took them off the ferris wheel. Every ten or twelve years, a new generation of younger customers comes into the fold. In theory, that means my grandson, who is now 14, will see things that to him are new, whether it's a vest, a double-breasted suit, an unconstructed garment, whatever. To him these styles are new, even though they've been around for many years. You have to keep in the back of your mind that there are always new generations. The older guy, he's been through all that. You're really catering to the younger blood, who bring a new fashion direction.

I like it still. I like fashion. I like color. The business is much more difficult now. Macy's bought the May Company, Belk's bought Profits, McRae's and Parisian. There is a lot of consolidation, so there are fewer people to sell. It makes the business more difficult, but you can still prevail if you have the right look, the right fashion at the right price, and a *raison d'être*. Many department stores are doing their own manufacturing, but they still have to come to the creative force of the industry because they can't possibly cover all the bases. They have to utilize outside talent to round out their own in-house talent. That is what's happening now. It's definitely a more difficult climate.

I have some regrets. I think that the launching of the Adolfo line, which is successful, could have been more successful, had we been more protective of distribution. In other words, there are brands out there today, they sell everybody, all the discounters. That is not the way to develop a brand with a lot of integrity. In theory, you want to sell Saks, Neiman Marcus, Bergdof Goodman. But in business, sometimes, there are downtrends. When you get hit with a downtrend and an off-price distributor of merchandise, like Syms or Burlington, comes your way, you might succumb to taking some business from them. When you do this, you are not maintaining the full integrity of the product or the brand. However, it's an accepted state of affairs nowadays.

I feel proud of the loyalty and friendships I've developed with many people who have worked for me. Over the course of 50 years, I've had people working for me for long stretches. My father hired one young lady, Eve Papageorge, in 1959, the year before he died. She was a very young lady. We didn't know it, but she wasn't even the legal age to work. She worked for us until about 1999. She is very bright and was always a dedicated and loyal employee. She also became a good friend, a relationship that we have maintained.

One of the first fellows I hired when my father died was Harvey Keenan, who was originally a customer. I liked him a lot. We became real friends and then he started to work for me. He stayed with our company for about 24 years. I've had a lot of people like that, people who've worked for me for 20, 25 years. We've all maintained the friendships. These were very nice men and women. My secretary, Andrea Isaacs, worked for me for probably 20 years. She is a very fine human being, was always caring and concerned, and was always there when needed. My cousin, Andre Milgram, worked for me for about 30 years. He helped coordinate overseas and domestic production. Unfortunately, he recently became ill. We wish him a speedy recovery.

My brother Gary was very involved with me from 1961 until 1990. He was a very good asset, very involved with the business. He then had an opportunity to get involved with a vitamin company, Nu Skin, a major multi-billion dollar company, and he's been involved with them since 1992. But during the years he was here, he was very helpful, instrumental in building the business. We had our differences, but we always worked them out. My mother was also involved in the business. From the time my father died in 1960, until 1990, when she moved to Florida, she was the production manager. She had a very good head on her. She was very helpful, right up until she became ill.

I have sometimes wished I was in something else. I was not sophisticated enough as a young man to understand real estate. In the little experience I've had in the last 20 or 30 years, I've learned that with a lot less effort, real estate has the long-run potential to be far more lucrative. Fashion is rewarding, but less so financially. For example, when you make a suit, the cost could be $150. You sell it, say, for $225, but if it hangs in your stock for a year, that suit is now worth maybe $75. A piece of real estate that you paid a million dollars to get, if you have it for ten years, all of a sudden, it's worth ten million dollars. It's a whole different equation. It's a different business, very interesting. If I were starting all over again, I would definitely look at the prospect of real estate as something very special.

The apparel business is more rewarding from a creative standpoint, from the point of view of accomplishment. When you make a collection and it goes out on the runway and everyone applauds, as I said earlier, it's like Broadway. You're getting acclaim from your peers. When the customers buy it, and it then performs at retail, which means the consumer is happy with it, then you know you've had a successful Broadway show. That's very satisfying.

In real estate, you don't worry about the color. You just worry about the nuts and bolts, the expenses, taxes, the rent roll, and the returns. The way the market has been for the last 40 years, it's really proven a very unusual situation. My friend's father built a complex of about 1800 apartments in the early 1940s or 1950s. He just sold that complex for one hundred and eighty million dollars. Which means the appreciation of 1800 apartments was unbelievable. This could never happen in the apparel business. It's almost like my home in Great Neck. I bought it in 1966. Forty years later, the monetary value of that home has appreciated 18-fold. That wasn't because I was so astute. I moved in, I lived there, and the real estate values just went up. The same principle was applicable 40 years ago. If I weren't making suits, if I were making buildings, it would be a similar appreciation. However, even in real estate, there are cycles, ups and downs. The key is to have staying power, to be able to weather the down times, in order to reap the benefits when the market regains its strength. I think about these things.

My friend, Shelly Fireman, was in the garment business, but eventually he opened up a restaurant in the Soho area called The Hip Bagel. He used to stay behind the counter. His idea was, instead of McDonald's with a hamburger roll, he figured he'd take a bagel and put a hamburger in it. From that, he built one restaurant and then another and now he has many. When he first opened up his restaurants, he was looking to take some people in as partners. Being a lifelong friend, I agreed to go in. I became a small partner in three restaurants, the Trattoria del'Arte, Redeye Grill, and the Brooklyn Diner. They are really good investments. One thing for sure, I get a table every time I walk into any one of those restaurants!

We get a return, but more important is the table (*laughs*). Although, seriously, they are very successful restaurants with big returns. The investors got a very nice return. So that's how I ended up in the restaurant business. The only thing is, I'm not the restauranteur. I don't stay in the kitchen and talk to the chef.

I've also had various real estate ventures that were not as successful as they should have been. I didn't have the foresight. In the early 1970s, my father had passed away, and my mother's second husband, Willie Windman, bought a brownstone, Central Park West at 74th Street. I think we paid about $150,000. Every year I used to get a call, my stepfather would say to me, "We need another $25,000."

After three years, I said, "This is the real estate business? I invested to get a return. Why am I still putting money in?"

After four years, I said, "Let's sell." I wanted out.

Which shows you how sophisticated I was, because three years later, they sold the same brownstone for close to a million dollars, and the guy who got it for a million sold it for four million. So over a period of ten years, I lost four million dollars because I wasn't sophisticated enough in real estate. Lessons to be learned.

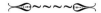

From 1952, until now, 59 years later, mine has definitely been a success story, but there were bumps along the road. There were definitely obstacles and difficult moments. Somehow, through drive and tenaciousness, I was able to bring the business out of a difficult period and move it forward. Difficult times were somewhat discouraging, but I was never discouraged. There is the Frank Sinatra song in which he sings, *I was down in May, but I was up in June. That's life!* I sing Frank Sinatra songs. One of my mottos is, *I did it my way.* ✷

Hard at work at the showroom office, 1290 Avenue of the Ameircas, New York City, 1991.

Just married! June 26, 1960.

A LEGACY
OF LOVE:
FAMILY

Courtship and Marriage

I started NYU in 1949. I immediately joined a fraternity called A E Pi. The fraternity house was on 10th Street and University place. I met a girl, Lynn, whom I dated from 1952 to 1956. We were quite serious and almost got engaged. Of all the women in my life, she was the one who was madly in love with me. But I was somewhat of a confused young man. I didn't know if I wanted to get married. I didn't want the responsibility. I dated her from the ages of 22 to 26. She lived in Brooklyn and came from a nice, hard-working family. It went so far that her family invited my parents for dinner. They were sort of pushing us to marry, the way parents will when their daughter is seriously dating a fellow.

I went through a very tough period. She was wonderful, but you might say I had mixed emotions. I spent a lot of time with her. I felt quite bad when we broke up because I knew she was very hurt, but I really didn't think she was the right match for me. If she should happen to read this book, I hope she is well and has had a good life.

I met another girl whose name was Joan and we dated for six months or a year. She was very nice, but she wasn't quite right, either.

In the summer of 1958, a couple of friends and I decided to go to a very exclusive summer resort called the Lake Tartleon Club. This was a very famous, hip place for supposedly upscale girls and guys. It was in New Hampshire. We immediately met some very wild girls and hung around with them for three days, but after that, I knew that they weren't for me. They were just not a right match, you might say.

I was standing around with my friends, Ira Howard, who was the editor of Cashbox, a music magazine, and Marvin Anklow, a friend from the garment center. We only had a couple of days left at the resort. We spotted these two girls who looked completely out of character for the place. They were very tall, slim, with beautiful blue eyes. They popped out of the whole crowd. Ira knew one of them, Linda, from the garment district. He said to her, "Do you have any rich friends?"

She said, "Well, I happen to be with a girl called Rene. Her family's wealthy. Do you know any rich guys?"

"Yeah," he said. "I'm with a friend. His name is Paul." No last names.

So there was an exchange. Ira introduced me to Linda and Linda introduced Ira to Rene. We all went out that evening to watch a show. It was like the Borscht Belt – comedians, maybe a singer – that kind of entertainment. That is how I met my future wife, although of course I didn't know that at the time. She was a very nice girl. That first night, we danced and had dinner.

When she met me, she said, "What's your name?"

I told her my name was Paul Paris. Don't ask me why! That's what it was. I adopted the name from my father's company, *Leon of Paris*. Since I'm French, it seemed like a more glamorous way of meeting a woman.

She said, "Where are you from?"

"Lower Westchester," I said.

I would not tell her I was from the Bronx. In those days, the Bronx wasn't such a high-class area. If you lived in Westchester, that was really something. If you lived in Riverdale, you were still okay. But if you lived in the Bronx, that was no big deal. Ira kept quiet and didn't say a word, except that he, too, was from "Lower Westchester."

The next morning, the four of us met up for a date. I was trying to impress her. I was somewhat of a waterskier, or, at least, I thought I was good. I said, "Why don't we go waterskiing?"

"Okay," she said. We all went out on the boat. When it was my turn to waterski, as luck would have it, I fell off the skis and they hit me on the head. I was bleeding. I was like a cripple! That was not too good an impression. You can imagine how I felt.

The next day, Ira told me that he had fallen in love with Rene. This was the girl of his dreams. Me, I still had that hang-up – I'm not taking any girl too seriously – having recently come out of all these romantic entanglements. I liked Linda. She was a nice girl, but I wasn't getting married the next day.

Before we had left for this little vacation, I had a discussion with my dad. I was already helping him with the manufacturing. We had a customer in Springfield, Massachusetts, which was located between New Hampshire and New York. He said to me, "On the way home, if you are going to that area, take with you a few samples and swatches."

In the garment business, you need to have a sample garment with you to show the potential customer. You also need some swatches to show them the different colors. Bring along an order book and you're in business.

I told my father, "Fine."

After a couple of days, Ira and I said goodbye to the girls, who were staying for another four or five days. Ira was already getting married. On our way back to New York, we stopped off at the customer's store, which was called Bontex Clothes. This was the hot store in Springfield. The owner was a guy named Steve Resnick. He had two stores and he was a real promoter. I showed him some swatches and he took a couple of orders. He took us to lunch. My friend, Ira, said, "I'd like to know where there's a florist around here."

Steve said, "What do you need a florist for?"

"I met a girl at the Lake Tartleon Club," Ira said. "She is the girl of my dreams. We're getting married. I want to send her a dozen roses."

Linda and my first photo together, the day we met. Lake Tarleton Club, July, 1958.

Steve said, "Fine. But, you know, I met my wife during the Depression. I didn't have money for roses. I went to the vegetable store. I
got her a stalk of celery for a nickle. Then I walked into the Mobil station and got a map, which was free. On the map, I wrote to my current
wife: I love you, Steve. I put a stalk of celery in the map, wrapped it up
and gave it to her. That's how we fell in love."

I listened to this story. Here my friend was sending a dozen roses. I
thought, *How will I look in this Linda's eyes? He's sending roses. I have to send*
something. I liked Steve's idea. I went to a vegetable store and bought a
stalk of celery for about a dime. I got a map and wrote on it, *Dear Linda,*
Great meeting you. Love you, Paul. I wrapped it up and sent it to her.

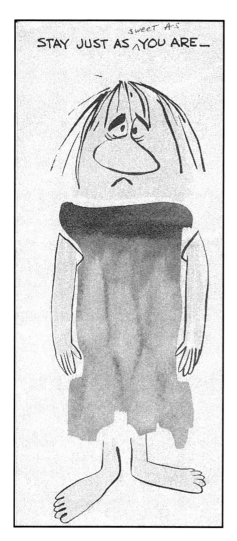

Card I gave to Linda with a stalk of celery, 1958.

She flipped out. She thought I was a terrible person, very cheap, which I probably was! My friend, Ira, he sent a dozen roses. His love was burning.

When Linda came back from New Hampshire, she told her mother she had met Paul Paris from Lower Westchester. Linda was only 18 or 19 at the time. Her father had just died. Her mother said, "Oy, You're so naïve. There's no such thing as Lower Westchester. And you think he's a Jewish boy with the name Paul Paris? What kind of name is Paris? You got totally fooled. I shouldn't have let you go to New Hampshire."

This was the first time her mother had let her go by herself. Mothers are naturally very protective of their daughters, and they were especially protective back then.

My friend Ira was madly in love. As soon as the girls got home, he wanted to call them. But in those days, to go from the Bronx to Brooklyn by subway was a strategic impossibility. On the other hand, I had a car.

Ira called me and said, "How would you like to go to Brooklyn?"

I said, "Argh." To get to Brooklyn in the days before major highways took at least an hour and a half, even just to get to King's Highway.

He said, "You've got to do me this favor. I've got to see this girl. We're in love."

I said okay. I called Linda.

She said, "Is your name Paul Paris?"

I said, "Well, yeah, that's my name."

"You're not really Paul Paris."

"No," I said. "It's Paul Wattenberg." She got a little upset about that.

"You live in Lower Westchester?"

"No, I live in the Bronx."

She was angry at first, but I was a good-looking young guy and she was a pretty gal and we had gotten along pretty well together. We made a date. Ira and I went to Brooklyn. He was supposedly getting married, after all. I was just along for the ride.

Then Ira and his girl broke up, while Linda and I started to date seriously. We had an interesting romance. We spent a lot of time together, even though she was in Brooklyn. We eventually got to the point where

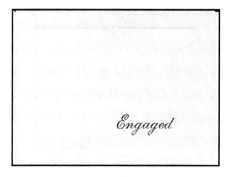

Engagement announcement, September, 1959.

I would sleep at her house because it was so impossible to get there. It was like going out of the country. Her father had died and she was living with her aunt Sylvia, her uncle Milton, and her mother Toby near Ocean Parkway.

Of course, here we are 49 years later. But we didn't get married for a couple of years. I still had that syndrome: I'm not sure. Do I really want to get married? I was very ambivalent.

I thought, Why am I rushing? even though I was already 26 years old when I met her and she was 19. We dated for two and a half years, until I was almost 29 and she was almost 22. We had an off-and-on relationship. At one point, the other girl I used to date called me and we almost got back together, but I realized she wasn't the right one for me.

Our romance became particularly rocky towards the end because I still wasn't sure that I wanted to get married. One time, we seriously broke up and I really missed her. I suddenly felt that she might really be the right girl, that she *was* the right girl. I got very excited. I called her and she said, "I can't see you. I met somebody else and I'm dating him."

That blew me out of the water. I said, "Let's talk."

That's one of my famous lines.

She didn't want to talk, but we finally did. I believe we got engaged at this reunion, which was probably in October or November. I told my parents. I didn't have any funds at the time, so my father bought the engagement ring. My father loved Linda. He thought she was wonderful, a very sensitive and caring human being. My mother loved her, too. My parents made us an engagement party in the Bronx. This must have been in 1959. We had her family, our family, all our close friends, the usual. It was an exciting moment. I was very excited about being in love with Linda and spending the rest of my life with her. We truly loved being together and engaging together in all kinds of mutual activities.

Then my father died on January 16, 1960. His sudden illness was a devastating emotional experience, followed by a long grieving period. Linda helped me a great deal through this terrible time. I needed a support system. She was with me at all times. Her love and caring lifted me out of my depression.

We had set a date to get married, June 26th, 1960. We set the date before my father died, to give him something to look forward to. I was excited about getting married, of course, but because of his passing, there

Engagement party, Bronx, November 1959.

Family reunion, November, 1959.

Gary, my parents and me at family reunion.

Family reunion, November, 1959. Standing, rear: My mother's cousin.
Middle row: Aunt Sally, my mother, my father, Aunt Toby, me, Uncle Isaac
Front: cousin Harry, Linda, cousin Ronald, cousin Betty and cousin Andie.

My father and mother, 1958.   Wedding kiss, June 26, 1960.

was a certain somberness about the wedding. It was both a very sad moment and a very happy moment. I walked down the aisle with my
mother and my brother, one on each side. My father wasn't there. It was
very bittersweet.

The wedding was not big. Linda's father had also died, but her
mother was wonderful. Together with Linda, she planned our whole
wedding day. We married in Temple Beth-El in Lawrence, Long Island.
Linda's sister, Marcia, was living in Hewlitt in a beautiful house, so we
had the wedding reception at her home. The weather was perfect, so it
was indoors and outdoors on the lawn. We had our parents' close friends
and our close friends. It was not fancy or elaborate, but at that particular time, we did what was appropriate. Our wedding day was very special and exciting.

A Family of Five: Moments to Celebrate

Three of the most exciting highlights of my life were when my children Lee, Debbie and Wendy were born. That was an absolute thrill. We had all three children – truly a gift – within the scope of five years.

The birth of each child was a very special moment in our lives. Each time you have a child, it's a mitzvah and a miracle, a very precious gift. Each child brought his or her unique personality, their very being, into the family circle. They each also brought to our family special luck and *nachas*, joy.

We were living in Forest Hills during the years our children were born. We moved to Great Neck in 1967, where we raised them.

Our first-born was a son, born November 15, 1961, and it created lots of excitement and joy. We named him Lee Adam and as I held him in my arms for the first time, I realized what a miracle and joy the birth of a child was for Linda and myself. It has been almost 50 years since Lee was born, yet I vividly remember that day as if it were yesterday. The excitement, the joy, the pleasure was beyond description. The last 49 years have certainly passed quickly. We have all shared lots of love, caring and many special moments and events. Lee was six years old when we moved to Lake Success in Great Neck. He attended Parkville public school and then moved on to Great Neck South. He was a good student. He excelled, however, in lacrosse and baseball. He played lacrosse extremely well for the Great Neck South team. As for baseball, I recall attending his Little League games and being impressed by his ferocious tenacity as catcher. No matter how much bigger the opposing runner sliding into home plate, Lee would assiduously guard the plate and be sure that the runner was out.

Murray Eisen and Lee, me and David Cooper with sailfish Lee caught, Acapulco, 1978.

Lee and me in front of my yacht, *The Frenchman*, July, 1979.

As Lee approached his thirteenth birthday, he aggressively studied his Haftorah portion. At his Bar Mitzvah service in synagogue, he read it exceptionally well and made us all very proud. His reception was at the Plaza Hotel in New York City. What a great party it was – an evening never to be forgotten. Linda and I had a very small wedding because my father had just died, so Lee's Bar Mitzvah reception was like a "coming out" party for us.

As time marched on, Lee graduated from Great Neck South and chose to attend Syracuse University. Four years later, we all attended Lee's graduation from Syracuse with honors. He worked the following summer at our company *Leon of Paris/Adolfo* in men's apparel. He adapted quickly to the industry. He was a quick learner, with a flair for style and fashion. As I traveled throughout Europe to fabric shows and factories, Lee accompanied me and learned all aspects of the men's apparel business from A to Z. In the early eighties, he experienced the transition from domestic to overseas manufacturing. The dynamics changed and the American manufacturing companies could not compete in the world's international markets. The choice was difficult, but obvious: it was necessary to manufacture overseas in order to stay in business. Lee adapted quickly and well. We organized a complete import company, of which he is the CEO and president today. For the last 20 years, he has proven to be a good leader and businessman.

Lee's life had a dramatic change. He met Laura in June, 2000 and a short time later, they had a real surprise wedding. On a Sunday afternoon, he told Linda and I that the wedding was taking place the following Saturday. We were all pleasantly surprised and shocked. All was set. The only thing we had to do was attend. All of Lee's and Laura's friends and family were in attendance. The wedding was small, but had all the bells and whistles: the music, the rabbi to officiate, the flowers, the food, the photographer and the beautiful decor. Their wedding was perfect, a truly euphoric and memorable event.

Lee and Laura's wedding, April 28, 2001.

Lee and Laura were blessed shortly thereafter with two amazing children, Ethan and Dylan. Lee's focus and life have completely changed. He is a wonderful father, husband, son and a very good businessman. Most important are his sensitive and caring ways. He is always there when needed. He is very involved in both of his children's sports and activities. Ethan plays hockey, soccer, basketball, and baseball. Dylan is on a swim team, does ballet and gymnastics, and plays soccer and basketball.

On a personal note, Lee and I have worked alongside each other for 28 years. We have had our differences on how aspects of the business should be run. However, whatever controversies occur during the work day or week, the next day or week, we are still bonding. As time goes on, I have Lee make most of the day-to-day decisions. We still have controversies, but fewer and fewer each day. For me to let go has been a challenge, but after 58 years in the men's apparel business, I recognize it is time to let go and let Lee lead and be the CEO of our company. I am sure he will continue to be successful as he is immensely creative and talented. His capacity to do things is sometimes overwhelming and goes beyond what anyone would expect from one person.

Our first daughter, Debra (Debbie) was born on January 25, 1963 and it was truly a very momentous occasion. She was a beautiful baby. I recall in the hospital holding this new and very special treasure. It is now 47 years later and never in our wildest thoughts and dreams could we have imagined all the most unusual and special accomplishments Debbie would attain. As a student in the Parkville public school, she continuously earned high grades and was among the top ten students in her group: smart, clever and very involved in all school activities. In sports, she was a quick and outstanding track star for Great Neck South. She also excelled in tennis. I can't forget her ballet dancing and gymnastics. She was immensely focused and excelled in each and every undertaking. Her

Bat Mitzvah was spectacular and she, too, did exceptionally well reading the Haftorah. She was very well-versed in her Bat Mitzvah speech.

How proud Linda and I were when Debbie graduated from Great Neck South with many honors.

Her next step was the University of Michigan in Ann Arbor. During her Michigan studies, it appeared that she had her heart set on medicine. Her graduation from university with honors was again that focused little girl who was now on her way to a possible career in medicine. I recall meeting Debbie and we spoke about her being accepted in the Mount Sinai medical curriculum. Since Debbie and her fiancé were engaged, staying in New York was very important to both of them. After medical school at Mount Sinai, Debbie's outstanding grades enabled her to be accepted and given one of the very few seats in the residency program in

Debbie's graduation from University of Michigan, 1983.
l to r: 2nd from left — Debbie, Brett Rosen, Linda, me, and Wendy.

dermatology in Mt. Sinai Medical School. The rest speaks for itself. Debbie is now a professor at Mt. Sinai. She entered private practice about 20 years ago and moved to 69th Street and 5th Avenue where she opened her own private practice office in dermatology and surgery about 10 years ago. I am proud that she has become an exceptionally talented dermatologist with a great following. It's hard to believe that it is 47 years since the little baby girl grabbed my finger with her tiny, little hand.

Her accomplishments keep amazing Linda and me. In the last few years, Dr. Debra Wattenberg's appearances on NBC's "The Today Show" have become a regular occurrence, consulting on dermatology matters (including controversial dermatological issues). Her television presence is seen coast to coast. Her TV appearances are always special and Linda and I are so proud as we watch our baby (Dr. Daughter) answer questions about dermatology for viewers from all over the United States.

Now let's turn to her personal life accomplishments. She married Brett Rosen (her childhood sweetheart) in 1985 at the Plaza Hotel in a fairy-tale wedding. That was some evening. Her ceremony was in the Terrace Room. The reception was in the Grand Ballroom. Watching her come down the steps was enchanting. We pulled out all the stops, whether it was flowers, music, anything and everything. It was a magical evening. Her husband, handsome Brett Rosen, made the evening complete. Brett has been a great addition to our family. While building her medical career, Debbie gave birth to our first granddaughter, Jamie (who was just accepted to medical school). Then came Rachel, a brilliant scholar and our second granddaughter, who will graduate next June from Dalton High School with spectacular honors. I am sure she will attend a top college. Her athletic skills in soccer and basketball are excellent. Then came Kyle, our grandson, who is also brilliant and sophisticated, not to mention a good golfer, soccer player, lacrosse and baseball specialist.

Debbie and Brett's wedding, June 21, 1986.

Debbie and Brett and their family engage in many unorthodox events. Two years ago, as a family, they all went to New Zealand to sky-dive! Linda and I were certainly against this event. However, they did it and thank God all are okay and I believe they will not go sky-diving again.

In a few, short years, Debra has gone beyond our dreams. Most special are her caring and concerned ways as daughter, mom, and wife. She is also superbly organized. How she does it all is beyond comprehension.

Our third child (and second daughter) Wendy was born on December 3, 1965. It was a great blessing to have such a beautiful baby with lots of black hair and sparkling blue eyes. The moment she wrapped her little fingers around my index finger, I knew a special connection had just occurred. Wendy was the baby and always in the forefront of all family affairs. I recall the great thrill for Lee and Debbie when we brought her home, their baby sister. She was the novelty and loved by all. She has always been as nice as a human being can possibly be. Like sugar, she is very sweet.

When we moved to our Lake Success home, Wendy was two and a half years old. Shortly thereafter, she attended Parkville kindergarten. Time passed quickly and she attended Great Neck South High School. She promptly became active in sports. She was on the track team and fast. She was then selected to join the school cheerleading team. At all games, as a cheerleader she was popular, beautiful and the best in her group. While in high school, she was a star on her gymnastics team. She scored lots of points for the Great Neck South High School team.

Wendy also had a beautiful Bat Mitzvah. It was not officially in the temple, but we did it in a special catering hall. Her party was a smash. It had a Western theme, and was spectacular, with all of her friends present.

Our home in Lake Success was a continuous center of activities and social get-togethers amongst our three children and their friends. Wendy grew up fast and made us proud with her outstanding achievements in sports and

Wendy and Steven's wedding, October 27, 1990.

in academics. When Debbie left for Michigan University and Lee for Syracuse, Wendy kept our house alive and active. She graduated from Great Neck South High School with honors and got accepted to the University of Pennsylvania. However, she ended up at Michigan University. Four years passed quickly and how proud we were as Wendy graduated with honors. Upon her return from Ann Arbor, she was accepted at Saks Fifth Avenue into their Executive Training Program. In the meantime, she met, dated, and married Steven Gottfried. Their wedding at Fresh Meadow Country Club in October was like a dream. It had all the bells, whistles, flowers, and music one could have wished for. A really fun aspect was the attendance of their dog, a golden retriever, who was in many pictures. What followed was really magical. Steven and Wendy had three sons Ryan, Cory, and Andrew. The boys and the family became a dedicated hockey family. The parents travel coast to coast with all three sons.

Along with being a homemaker, hockey mom, all-around mother and wife, several years ago Wendy became the Executive Vice-President and General Merchandise Manager at Saks Fifth Avenue, which is a huge accomplishment. Both highly professional and successful, she is well-recognized by management and her peers. How she does it all is amazing. Perhaps most special is that she is a most loving, caring wife, mom and daughter and she is always there when anyone needs her. How she does it all boggles the imagination. Wendy is truly in a league all her own.

I'm very proud of all of them. They are an amazing group, and have brought Linda and I only *nachas* – joy – throughout the years.

I think I always expressed my love for my children. To this day, I don't think they have any doubt about it. There isn't anything I would not do for them. I am always there for them, no matter what their needs or requirements might be. I do that for my wife and my grandchildren, as well.

Wendy, Lee and Debbie,

From the moment you were all born, the three of you became the focal point of my existence. Your smiles were the sunshine in my heart. Your happiness was the only treasure I sought. All three of you should know that when each one of your tiny hands touched mine, I knew then that I had been chosen to nurture you, love you and give you the strength to let go.

Debbie, Wendy and Lee, c. 1984.

Letting go of all three of you was not easy, but I look at you all now. Two beautiful young women and a handsome man. Each one of you strong in your individual convictions and determined to face life on your own terms.

My dreams for your life might not always be the same ones you seek. But one thing remains the same for all three of you: your happiness, love, and caring will always be my greatest treasure. I look back and reflect on that first touch when each of you were born. I now know that the true miracle of that first touch is revealed in one simple truth: even though your hand may slip away from mine, we will all hold each other in our hearts forever.

Dad

Our Children's Spouses

Brett Rosen is not our son-in-law. To Linda and me, he is our son. Brett and Debbie are soon to celebrate their 25th wedding anniversary. Brett is a wonderful husband, father and a good friend to many. He is also very bright, very ambitious and very successful, with a multi-faceted career. A professional estate planning expert, he also recently became a partner at a well-respected bond trading and consulting company called Edgewealth Management. Brett is well-respected by business associates, friends and family. He also shows special dedication as a father, always involved with Jamie's, Rachel's and Kyle's sports and education. He is there to teach them, cheer them on and, when needed, to discipline them. As a husband, he is caring, loveing, and always supportive of Debbie's feelings and needs. His devotion to the Oxalosis and Hyperoxaluria Foundation for kidney research is a very special trait that he possesses. His relentless efforts on behalf of that organization are extraordinary. In the last few years, he has made a super-human effort, including participating in a triathalon, to raise funds so that a cure will be found.

Steven Gottfried is also not our son-in-law. He is another son to Linda and myself. Steven is president of the Service Channel, which is a computer concept that he created, developed and has now built into a major company. His clients include the Who's Who in the American retail scene from coast to coast. Steven's level of energy, drive and ambition is surreal. He often travels along the width and breadth of the United States, visiting and soliciting new and potential clients. However, no matter where in the country he may be, he always makes it his special responsibility to be home so he can participate and take his sons Ryan, Cory and Andrew to their respective hockey or soccer tournaments together with Wendy. At times, he may have jet-lag or be tired, but he is always there for his family. He is a caring and loving father, son and husband. He is always available when needed and totally devoted to his family.

Laura, who is married to our son, Lee, is our daughter. Period. She is a breath of fresh air as an addition to our family. She is a great mother, wife, and daughter. She is lovable, caring and always there when needed. She is also very bright and energetic. As a career, she heads up a division of a large family sprinkler installation corporation, which is very successful. They have recently signed contracts to install sprinklers in the new Twin Towers that are being rebuilt in New York City. As a wife, she is very caring, attentive, and loving to Lee and to the whole family. She and Lee attend all of Ethan's hockey, basketball, baseball, and soccer games. She also attends all of her daughter Dylan's ballet dances and swim meets. Between the two of them, they attend all their children's sports activities. As a daughter, Laura is also always there for her own mother. She is a great homemaker and totally devoted to her family, and is simply an all-around fantastic human being.

Linda's Career

My wife has been an entrepreneur for 40 years. She always worked. She is artistically inclined. She first went into a joint venture with a group of her friends. They opened a tapestry store. Linda was the artist of the group. She sketched the paintings that the girls would copy onto the tapestry.

I was supportive of her working, but I did not encourage her to work in New York City. I felt that the children needed their mother. To me, that was the number one priority because I wasn't as readily available as I thought I should be. I felt, *How can I let her work and the two of us will be away from the children?* We made a compromise. Since we lived in Great Neck, she would open up her store in Roslyn, which was 20 minutes away. She could go to work in the morning after the kids went to school and be home by 3:00 when the kids came home. In this way, she would always be there for them.

She must have been in that business for about five years. It was a successful venture. They made a profit. But then she got sick. The paints she was using emitted a chemical vapor which was damaging her lungs. She and her friends had to give up the business.

Her next venture was a ladies' boutique in Great Neck that she opened up with her best friend, Judy Myers. They called it *Deux Amie.* Linda did the merchandising and the buying. She is very talented and her taste level is beyond compare. She and Judy worked really hard and spent a lot of time at the store. In retail, you have to put in Saturdays, which can be a real pain in the neck. We belonged to a country club. My wife is a tennis player and she wanted to play on the weekends. Luckily, Judy did not play tennis and was kind enough to be in the store on Saturdays while Linda played for a couple of hours. The store was successful, but after five or six years, the thrill of being in business wore off, and they closed.

Between the tapestry business and *Deux Amie,* I guess she must have spent between 10 and 12 years in business.

She then began a home-based business, building jewelry boxes made out of seashells. She eventually expanded her repertoire and designed antique costume jewelry. She exhibited her work at shows at the Armory in New York City. She did that for about four or five years.

Of the 40 years we were married, I would say that for 20 years she was involved in something entrepreneurial. She always kept herself busy. She liked the challenge. It wasn't a question of money; my business was doing pretty well. I didn't need her income to maintain our lifestyle. The money she earned was extra, pin money that she could spend as she pleased to go shopping, give to the children, or do as she liked.

Linda has always been there for me. She is a wonderful mother and grandmother. She is a premier wife, as good as it gets – caring, sensitive, lovable, talented, and supremely family-oriented.

My Mother's Later Years

My mother remarried in the 1970s. Remember, my father died in 1960, at the age of 51. My mother was only 49 years old at the time. Her second husband's name was Willy Windman. He was a real Holocaust survivor. He was in a concentration camp and survived, but he saw his whole family destroyed. He was a very dedicated Holocaust worker, an executive in the Miami Holocaust Foundation.

He was very good to my mother. They must have met in the 1970s. They traveled all over the world and had a good time together. At first, I was a little from the old-fashioned school regarding her getting married again. *He's not my father, how could you do this?* But after a while I accepted him because I saw how very good he was to her.

When she was 66, they went on a world tour together. They went to Tahiti, Australia, all over the Orient. At that time, there was a swine flu epidemic. My mother and her husband had a swine flu shot before they left, but when they came home, she called me and said, "You know, I can't move my legs."

My mother and her second husband, Willy Windman, 1966.

We rushed her to the hospital. She had a disease called Guillame-Barre. It's an allergic virus that attacks your nervous system. You become completely paralyzed, from your toes up. She was in the hospital for many weeks, while they had her on the heart-lung machine. She was in a coma for about three weeks. It was a very trying episode. I remember it like it was yesterday. One night, the doctor said to me, "I don't think she'll make it through the night."

We had a Rabbi Bauman at the Lake Success Jewish Center. I called him at 10:00 at night. I was hysterical. He said, "What's going on?"

"They said mom wouldn't live through the night. Would you mind opening the temple?"

He was nice enough to do it. We recited special prayers. It was a very religious moment. It was also a crazy thing to do. I sometimes do crazy things. We opened the Torah. I don't know how we did it. Some-

My mother, her sister Toby, my cousin Betty, and me, 1985.

My mother and me, 1988.

Dancing with my mother, c. 1988.

how we went to the temple and made a prayer of some kind. In my heart, I guess I'm a believer, even though my whole family got destroyed, which has made me a skeptic at times, too.

She didn't die. She came out of the coma and survived.

In these cases, the virus supposedly becomes dormant and then you are okay. But some people get residual damage, which is what happened to her. She ended up in a wheelchair for 14 years. She had a very tough time. She had women attendants 24/7 for all that time. Towards the end, she kept saying to me that she didn't want to live anymore. She was totally depressed and dejected and upset about her condition.

"This is no life," she said.

She had a rough time. But she was very courageous, even through that period. She tried very hard. We had her at Rusk Institute and then we took her to the Burke Institute in Westchester. She spent about eight months in both places. She had to learn how to write all over again, because of the damage. They taught her how to feed herself. She almost started walking. Fourteen years is a long time to be entrapped in your own body. It was a very sad thing. She was six weeks shy of her 80th birthday when she died in 1990.

When she got sick, we were thankful for her new husband. He stuck by her, which was unusual. He was a very nice man. They were married for close to 20 years.

We were nice to him, too. My brother and I really took care of everyone as far as their financial needs and everything else. He died about fourteen years ago after bypass surgery. The surgery was successful, but afterwards, he got an infection in his throat where the intubator had been. When they removed the heart-lung machine, the infection was so bad that he never recovered. He was about 85. I gave a eulogy at his funeral. I thanked him.

Extended Family

I have my cousin Betty Milgram and her husband André here in the United States. My cousins Georges and Margot Bajczman were in Paris, although Georges recently passed away. Frida Wattenberg is in Paris. Cousin Jacques and his wife Lillian Wattenberg and my cousin Nicole and her husband and Roland, these are all my father's brother's children in Paris. Then there are the grandchildren. Alexandra Wattenberg, also in Paris. Anna and Emile Steinberger, who are my mother's sister's children, are in Houston, Texas. We keep in touch with the few remaining cousins on occasion, even though we are geographically in different locations. My mother's sisters and brothers and my father's brothers have all passed away. Time marches on.

Uncle Joseph, me and Uncle Maurice, c. 1999.

Cousins Andre and Betty Milgram, Georges and Margot Bajczman, 2002.

Linda and me with Margot and Georges Bajczman, Wendy's wedding, 1990.

Our Grandchildren

Of course, we have eight special blessings, our grandchildren. The first granddaughter is Jamie Rosen, who is now 20 and going to the University of Pennsylvania. Jamie is an all-around amazing athletic person. She plays soccer, basketball, lacrosse, and golf. She also plays piano. Her sister Rachel, who's 16, is involved in softball, soccer, lacrosse, and golf. She also plays the piano. Their brother Kyle is a great soccer player. He's an amazing all-around athlete – basketball, soccer, golf, you name it and he can do it. Last Sunday, he hit over 200 yards on the tee-off shot. He's only 13 years old. That is really amazing. He has a great swing. He is a very ambitious, very competitive, extremely bright and good-looking

Linda, me, Lee and grandchildren, 2005.

Ryan, Andrew and Cory.

Dylan.

young man. He also plays the guitar. He and his friends formed a band and they are truly good. He's really very diversified.

Wendy's children are also unusual. Ryan Gottfried, who is almost 17, is in high school. Ryan is a very special guy. He's an extremely affectionate, sensitive, caring human being. Ryan is involved in hockey and golf. They are a big hockey family. They really are fantastic hockey players and ice skaters and athletes. Cory, who is a most unusual little grandson — he's not so little, he's almost my height! — he was just 14. He is a sensational hockey player and he's also been scouted by the Islanders. He plays on their farm team. He's a spectacular defensive player. He also plays guitar, soccer, roller hockey, basketball, and golf. Andrew Gottfried is the youngest of Wendy's children. He's nine years old. He's really all-around. Again, a hockey player. We have a lot of hockey players and soccer players. Andrew also likes basketball and, recently, he has become very excited about golf. He's doing well!

All around, we've got a very musical and athletic family.

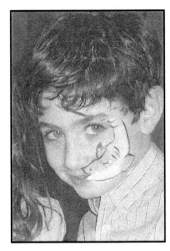

Ethan.

Jamie, Rachel and Kyle.

The new additions to the family are my son Lee's two children, who are like sugar and honey. Ethan Wattenberg is now seven years old. He's a very, very big sports fan. He loves soccer, basketball and baseball. He likes golf, too. He's going to be a good golfer. He's very aggressive and when he watches hockey or basketball, he knows every player, he knows how they score, he knows the position they play and he knows their name. Seven years old! He looks forward to every one of these sporting events on television and he goes to them. He likes baseball, too, and he goes to the games. Dylan, who's six years old, is like a fairy-tale little girl. She's very bright. She's tall and she's not yet into sports, but I'm sure she will be. She likes golf, but she hasn't really played it yet. She likes swimming. She'll get into soccer. She likes playing with dolls, as little girls would. She's very artistic. She likes to paint. She is the sweetest girl.

We had a great Bat Mitzvah for Jamie, a wonderful Bat Mitzvah for Rachel at Fresh Meadow Country Club and amazing Bar Mitzvahs for Kyle and Cory. We had a slightly smaller Bar Mitzvah for Ryan.

Jamie's Bat Mitzvah. Back l to r: Cory, Jamie, Ryan, Kyle.
Front l to r: Rachel and Andrew Fresh Meadow Country Club, 2002.

Cory's Bar Mitzvah. Top l to r: Rachel, Ryan, Cory, me, Linda, Jamie, Kyle.
Bottom l to r: Dylan, Ethan, Andrew. 2008.

Kyle's Bar Mitzvah, "The guys." Back l to r: Cory, Lee, me, Steven, Ryan. Front l to r: Ethan and Andrew. Fresh Meadow Country Club, 2008.

Kyle's Bar Mitzvah, "The gals." Back l to r: Debbie, Wendy, Laura, Linda. Front l to r: Rachel, Dylan, Jamie. Fresh Meadow Country Club, 2008.

Triple Bar Mitzvah. Kyle, Cory, Ryan. Jerusalem, August 2008.

Kyle, Cory and Ryan's triple Bar Mitzvah. Jerusalem, August 2008.

In August, 2008, the whole family went to Israel. We had a triple Bar Mitzvah for Kyle, Cory and Ryan in Jerusalem on August 21st. The whole experience had a mystical feel. All three grandsons recited their Haftorahs beautifully. We were 21 people in all, and we went to the Western Wall on a private bus, accompanied by two guides and an Israeli soldier as a guard for the whole trip. Wendy did all the planning. It was perfect except for the 100° heat during the day — that was a little tough. This is an experience that will be remembered forever.

As a tradition, Linda and I have created a special event. For each of our grandchildren, after their thirteenth birthday, we let them select a place to travel anywhere in the world (within reason! Not the Arctic Circle!)

For our first trip, we took our eldest granddaughter Jamie to London for about nine days. Every day with Jamie was an education. Our itinerary was filled with lots of special sights. We went to see how the English Parliament operates and debates the issues of the day. We watched Tony Blair debate his position on international politics. We visited the famous wax museum of Madame Tussaud. It was fun seeing the world's most famous celebrities in wax, but looking very real. We also visited the underground hideout where Prime Minister Churchill and the important government officials of the day were living and hiding during the Nazis' relentless bombing of London during World War II. Because of this underground hideaway, the British government was able to conduct their business and run the country during the Blitzkreig. We also attended British musical theater and saw *Chitty Chitty Bang Bang*. We went to Buckingham Palace, where Jamie enjoyed the changing of the guard. Viewing the British Queen's crown jewels and diamonds was an overwhelming experience. Linda and I enjoyed being with Jamie every moment. She was a complete pleasure the entire time. This is a trip that will never be forgotten.

Jamie's 13th birthday trip.
Linda, me, Jamie. London, 2001.

13th birthday trip for Rachel and Ryan.
Linda, Rachel, Ryan, me.
Venice, Italy. July 2006.

Our next thirteenth birthday trip for our grandsons Cory and Kyle is slightly delayed. It is only delayed, however. It will take place in the near future.

We took our second "thirteenth birthday" trip to Venice and Rome in July, 2005 with our grandson Ryan and our granddaughter Rachel. It was great to be alone with two special grandchildren for a very unique ten-day holiday. From New York, we landed near Venice which, with all its canals, was very charming. Our hotel was also quite charming. We had a suite with an extra room that the children shared. Each day we had a planned activity. We went sightseeing from our hotel via gondola to various historical art museums and sights. We visited the Venice Guggenheim Museum. A very unique experience was going to a world-renowned glass-making factory with a guide. We actually watched artisans glass-blowing and saw how they create some of the most famous art glass in the world. We also visited a Jewish neighborhood where one of the oldest synagogues in Venice still exists, having survived the Holocaust intact. Shopping was also a very important part of Venice. Ryan was very focused on sunglasses and watches, while Rachel was focused on the latest Italian fashions, having very good taste in clothes. We also visited several of Venice's most famous churches.

Our next stop was Rome. We stayed at the Hassler Hotel near the Spanish Steps. It was about 100° every day, which only slowed our sightseeing, but never stopped it, despite the heat and humidity. Going to old Rome (formerly Romano) was a special and interesting experience. The old amphitheater has been preserved and it is quite interesting to see what Rome looked like many years ago during the height of the Roman Empire.

Altogether, we did lots of sightseeing, going to museums, and shopping. Most memorable was being with Rachel and Ryan, both of whom were fun to be with. We also enjoyed the Italian lunches and dinners. Ten exciting days passed very quickly. We returned to New York a bit tired, but with wonderful memories. This trip is never to be forgotten. Ryan and Rachel: Linda and I loved every moment of being with you.

Family Trips

I think a very special tradition in my family is that every Thanksgiving for the last 15 years, we have taken the whole family away. We went to Jamaica and Puerto Rico. We took many, many trips to Florida. London. Venice. Rome. We went to Israel. We went to Paris, France. France was an amazing trip. We spent 10 days there. That was really special. We went to the Louvre Museum. We went to Versailles and we saw where the King and Queen slept. My grandson, Kyle, said, "Gee, there's no bathrooms here. How did they go to the bathroom?" It was the 17th century – I guess there was no plumbing!

I think those trips were something that everybody looked forward to. It was once a year that we'd all be together, which was a special event. We took spouses, grandchildren, everybody. Even when they were growing up, we always took the children. We went with the whole family.

For our most recent trip, to celebrate Linda and my 50th anniversary, we took the entire family for a glorious two-week "once-in-a-lifetime" trip to Italy and France. It all began in late 2009. Linda and I very much

Back l to r: Cory, Debbie, Linda, me, Wendy, Dylan, Steven, Laura, Lee
Front l to r: Brett, Jamie, Ethan, Andrew, Kyle.
Hermitage Hotel, Forte dei Marmi, Italy. August 2010.

Back l to r: Cory, Debbie, Linda, me, Wendy, Dylan, Steven, Laura, Lee.
Front l to r: Brett, Jamie, Ethan, Andrew, Kyle.
Hermitage Hotel, Forte dei Marmi, Italy. August 2010.

wanted to do something unusual for this special anniversary. We thought about making a big party, but that was ruled out. We thought about a family cruise, or maybe a safari, but the latter would entail way too many mosquitos. Since my heritage is French, we decided to try to get a house in St. Tropez, but could not get the perfect house for 16 people. Finally, we decided to go to Forte dei Marmi, Italy and Paris, France.

Organizing this trip to take place in August, 2010 was quite a challenge and involved lots of complicated logistics. With lots of planning and coordination, we were finally able to have all our children, their spouses and all eight grandchildren together in Forte dei Marmi, which is about 40 minutes from the Pisa Airport. We stayed at the Hermitage Hotel, which is very family-oriented, with a child-friendly atmosphere, situated right near the beach and the town. The combination of hotel, the

Back l to r: Mark, Steven, Lee, Jody, Lew, David, Laura, Debbie, Brett, Ryan.
Middle l to r: Wendy, Kyle, Jamie, Andrew.
Front l to r: Cory, Dylan, Linda, me, Ethan. Forte dei Marmi, Italy August 2010.

town and the marvelous white beaches with cabanas and all the facilities made it truly a great holiday for all.

On our first day, everyone in the family rented a bicycle. The beach was only a few blocks away, and the hotel's shuttle service made it easy to get back and forth. Lunches were served right on the beaches. Dinners for 16 to 20 people were arranged via our concierge with advanced planning.

Several highlights are worth mentioning. We went together as a family to Florence for a day of sightseeing, lunch and shopping. Even though Linda and I were a little tired, it was lots of fun, especially the museum which has the statue of David. It was a huge surprise when Shelly and Marilyn Fireman invited the entire family to their mountaintop home near Pietrasanta for a 50th anniversary luncheon. They were wonderful hosts.

"On the way to town on our daily mode of transportation." Linda and me, Forte dei Marmi, Italy. August 2010.

"Beach hat scene."
Cory, Kyle, Ryan and Andrew.
Forte dei Marmi, Italy. August 2010.

In front of "David museum".
Cory, Steve, me, Wendy, Brett, Ryan, Kyle, Rachel, Debbie. Florence, Italy. August 2010.

In front of "David museum" l to r: Cory, Steve, me, Wendy, Brett, Ryan, Kyle, Rachel, Debbie. Florence, Italy. August 2010.

Linda and my 50th anniversay luncheon at the mountaintop home of Shelly and Marilyn Fireman. Pietrasanta, Italy. August, 2010.

Shelly and me. Forte dei Marmi, Italy. August 2010.

Ponte Vecchio. Brett, Debbie, Steven, Wendy. Florence, Italy. August 2010.

Debbie, Jamie, Rachel, Brett and Kyle. Pietrasanta, Italy. August 2010.

Back l to r: Lee, Laura, me, Linda
Front l to r: Ethan, Dylan.
Paris, France, August 27, 2010.

In front of Sacré Coeur Church,
August 2010.

We all enjoyed visiting their beautiful home, along with the special treat of a delicious and gorgeous anniversary cake with all the trimmings.

The Hermitage Hotel was a perfect family-oriented setting. When Lee arrived a few days later and we were all together, our children made a surprise cocktail party that featured a 50th anniversary video in the hotel. The whole party was truly special with the wine, champagne and hors d'oeuvres, but the most euphoric moment was when our family showed Linda and me the video. They had compiled photos and live videos and set them to music, reflecting over 50 years of our family togetherness and various family highlights. As the video tape ended, it was surely a wonderful, emotional high point of our trip.

When Lee arrived, we were all together for three days. Then Debbie, Brett and their family left and, a few days later, Wendy, Steven and their family also had to leave. We then took Lee, Laura, Ethan and Dylan to Paris.

In Paris, we went sightseeing at the Louvre and the Pompidour Museums. Going to the top of the Eiffel Tower for Ethan and Dylan was very exciting, and they had a great view of Paris from the top. Lunch at the Butte Montmartre (the famous artist's area) was fun. We then visited the famous Sacré Coeur Church, which was directly adjacent to where we ate lunch.

Since we were in my birthplace of Paris, Ethan and Dylan asked where I had lived when I was born. We got a driver who took us over to 24 Rue Butte aux Caille (Street of Pigeons). My father had his first men's and ladies' custom made-to-order store at this address and we lived in the back of the store. To my great amazement, the building remains exactly as it was in 1933 (77 years ago!). Of course, my dad's store is now a nicely renovated up-to-date apartment. Visiting this place of my birth was a deeply emotional experience.

Dylan, Ethan and me.
Butte Monmartre, August 2010.

Dylan, me, Ethan. 24 Rue Butte aux Caille.
My first home. The entrance was the same
80 years later! Paris, France. August 2010.

Lee and me in front of my second childhood home.
20 Boulevard Magenta, Paris. August 2010.

Right next door is a café called Chez Paul. That was a strange coincidence. The owner of Chez Paul was standing in front of the café. He came over to say hello and was a very good host, offering us all a drink and the comfort of his café. It was lots of fun. We also visited my second childhood home on Boulevard Magenta, the house we were living in when we tried to escape Paris, but were captured. Returning to this home was also a very moving experience. During our four days in Paris, we also visited and had a family reunion with our cousins Margot, Frank, Nathaly, and their children. Regretfully, my cousin Georges had passed away recently. We all miss him dearly. I hope, somehow, maybe he will read my book.

After 14 glorious days, we took our flight back to New York. I was ecstatic that it turned out to be a trip of a lifetime, truly never to be forgotten.

I feel we're blessed. Everyone is doing well. We are lucky to have such a well-rounded family and such a close family. We are always together. We're always at events, whether it's Rosh Hashanah or Yom Kip-

pur or the summertime. Whatever the occasion, there is always a wonderful closeness.

~~~~~~~

Whenever I have a difficult day, I look at the family picture taken at Rachel's Bat Mitzvah which shows my children, their spouses, all eight grandchildren, and Linda and I, all in one photograph. No matter how difficult a day I have, I look at that picture and feel that nothing should bother me. I'm blessed. To see eight grandchildren is a blessing in and of itself, along with my three wonderful children, their spouses, and a special, caring wife. ✱

This is the photograph that cheers me up when I am sad.
Rachel's Bat Mitzvah. Back l to r: Steven, Wendy, Debbie, Brent, Lee, Laura, Linda, me.
Middle l to r: Ryan, Rachel, Jamie, Cory. Front l to r: Andrew, Dylan, Ethan, Kyle.
Fresh Meadow Country Club, 2006.

Debbie's wedding, June 21, 1986.

LINDA
WATTENBERG:
LIFE WITH PAUL

My mother, Toby, was a third-generation American. Her mother and grandmother were both born in the United States. Her father was in the clothing manufacturing business, ladies' clothing.

My father, David Newman, was from Austria. As a young man, he worked as a shipping clerk for my maternal grandfather in the ladies' clothing business. That's how my parents met. After they got engaged, he went into his own business.

My sister and I were brought up in Brooklyn. We were very fortunate in the way we were raised. We had a private school education and went to summer camps. I also enjoyed one year of junior college, a school outside of Philadelphia called Harcum.

I graduated high school at the age of 16 and wanted very much to go to the Parsons School of Design. Art was my whole love. I put together a huge portfolio to apply, and I was very excited when I got accepted. The problem was that I was dating a young man my parents did not approve of. They wanted to break up the affair. Before I knew it, my mother got the application for Harcum and had me packed up and shipped off. It was a junior college, more like a finishing school. I went under protest for a year.

I was 17 when my father died.

We were living in a big house, but my mother didn't want to stay there, so we took an apartment with my mother's sister, Sylvia, and her husband, Milton. They had no children. The four of us lived together. In July and August, we were busy packing up the house. By September, my mother didn't have the money for me to go back to college, so I got a job in the garment center. I worked there for about two years as an assistant buyer for ladies' clothes. During that time, I really didn't date. None of my friends were around because they were still in college. My life pretty much consisted of going to work and coming home. Living in the apart-

Miami, 1957.

ment, I had no room to do any art or anything with my art. It was pretty much a quiet life from the time I was 17 to 19.

A friend of mine said, "Why don't we go away?"

It was the end of June. My mother said, "I think that's a wonderful idea. You need to go away. I'll pay for it."

My friend and I decided to go to Lake Tarleton in Pike, New Hampshire. It was the first time I was to go away alone. We were basically two naïve girls.

We were very athletic and into tennis, swimming and waterskiing. I was sitting somewhere and met a young man. He was very handsome, sweet, a nice guy, and he was telling me he's a starving editor for a movie magazine. Well, I had just broken up with a fellow who was a starving, working guy. I said, "I'm looking for a guy with money."

You have more guts to say things when you're very young.

He said, "I have a friend I want you to meet."

I said, "I have a friend I want you to meet, too."

That night the four of us went out together. We were very, what you called in those days "Ivy League girls." We wore Bermuda shorts and white bucks, which are white, suede shoes. If you didn't wear bucks, you wore penny loafers. These boys were not "Ivy League." They wore pompadour hairdos and what we would have called Seventh Avenue clothes. Short-sleeve shirts, kind of like bowling shirts.

When I met Paul, he told me his name was Paul Paris and that he was from Lower Westchester. The next day, we all went waterskiing. Of course, Paul fell. He had told me how terrific and wonderful he was, but he fell right off his skis. He certainly made an impression. My thought was, *This guy's a real jerk.*

They left the next day, and Paul's friend sent my friend a dozen roses. Paul sent me a stalk of celery. Again I thought, *What a jerk.* When I got

Lake Tarleton Club, July 8, 1958.

home, I told my mother I met this guy, Paul Paris, who lived in Lower Westchester. My mother was so upset. She said, "Paul Paris – that can't be a real name. And Lower Westchester is the Bronx."

When you were a young girl growing up in Brooklyn, it was okay if you dated a guy from Westchester, a guy from Long Island, or a guy from Brooklyn. But never the Bronx! It was just not heard of in our circle. So my mother was very, very upset.

Well, he called that night because his friend was taking my friend out and he wanted to double-date. My friend said, "Come on, go along. You haven't been dating. Let's go."

I said okay. On the phone, I asked him, "What kind of story are you giving me? Lower Westchester is the Bronx and what is your last name?"

He told me his real name was Paul Wattenberg, but that he was born in Paris. So I told my mother and again she said to me, "He's giving you a story. He doesn't sound like he has an accent on the phone" – she had answered the phone – "but if you want to go out with him, go out with him as long as the four of you are together." So we went out.

They came to pick us up and now they had crew cuts, very short hair, very Ivy League. No more pompadours. The other guy was wearing white bucks. We went out and had fun that night.

After a few dates, my friend stopped seeing the other guy, but Paul kept calling me and we continued to go out. I was working in the city at the time. Paul would meet me on Friday nights and bring me one rose. Always one rose. We would go out to dinner and then he would take me back to Brooklyn. This went on for months. I started getting more and more interested.

He told me that he wanted me to meet his parents at their summer home. I had never met them before. I thought I was going to a beautiful summer home somewhere in upstate New York. I was so excited. I didn't know what to buy them, so I bought a five-pound box of Barton's Chocolate. Barton's Chocolate was like *the thing* to buy. It was the Rolls-Royce of chocolate candy and it came in a beautiful box.

When we arrived in the country and got out of the car, I saw that they were staying in a bungalow colony. I was snobby and brought up with, *What do you mean, a bungalow colony?* This was his summer home, this little, two-bedroom bungalow. I met his mother, his father, and his brother, who was maybe 14 years old. I wasn't much older than he was! When it came time to sleep, I had to sleep in the room with his brother! Paul slept in the living room. I thought I was going to a big, beautiful home up in the country and the woods, and it ended up being a bungalow.

The more interested I became in Paul, the more he slacked off. He just wasn't as interested. After about eight or nine months, my mother began to insist, "You can't keep going out with him. You're getting older. You should be looking to meet someone to marry and have children, a family. I want you to start dating."

My father wasn't around any more and my mother wasn't capable of giving me real security. I can't say she didn't like Paul. It was just the security issue. It may have been a little bit of a prestige issue, too.

I told Paul I wasn't going to see him, that I was going to start dating. Of course, he never said anything, so I started to see other people.

In the past, whenever Paul and I went out, we went to a certain club in New York at The Ambassador Hotel. It was very, very elegant, with a bar outside and a dining room inside. Paul and I would go with a group of his friends, and we would always stay outside by the bar. He didn't have the money to go inside for dinner.

When I started dating other boys, when they asked me where I wanted to go, if I knew a boy could afford it, I would say, "To the Ambassador Hotel, the Embassy Club." They'd say, "Sure, let's go have drinks and dinner there."

The first time I went to the Embassy Club with a date, Paul was there, sitting outside with his date and his friends. I knew he would be there because that was his thing, every Friday or Saturday night.

He saw me arrive with my date. We sat down outside at a table and had a drink. It was just the two of us. When we were finished, we went into the dining room and had dinner. Paul was shocked! Of course, the next day he called me. I said, "If you're not interested in anything serious, I'm still dating."

The next week, the other young man called and said, "Let's go back. I liked it." So we went back.

Paul called again. He would call me once a week, religiously. Sometimes, he called three or four times a week.

I started dating another young man. Three months later, he asked me to marry him, but I just wasn't sure. I hadn't dated anyone for the two years prior to meeting Paul, and it was now almost two years since Paul and I had met. I was 20 or 21.

When Paul made his weekly phone call, I said, "You have to stop calling. I am getting engaged."

He said, "Well, let's talk."

"No," I said. "Unless you have something to say, I have nothing to talk about."

I was much more interested in Paul than I was in the other fellow. He was more fun, he made me laugh. Being with him was just more exciting. But the other guy was so, so attentive. Paul had started off very attentive, with his rose every Friday, but as soon as I got interested, he wasn't around any more.

Finally, I said, "Okay, I'll meet you."

We went out for dinner. I said, "Look. I can't do this. I lied to Bob and told him I was going to do something with my mother. Instead, I'm having dinner with you. It's really absurd. If you're not interested in having a relationship – ".

"Well, we could live together."

"Nice girls don't live together," I said, "when they're 20 years old. Unless you're interested in getting engaged, having a family and going forward, good bye."

He said, "Well, okay."

We went back to my house. He went in and told my mother that he wanted to get married. He called his parents and told them. His mother got a little upset that he didn't tell her first, but his father was flying! He was so happy. His father loved me. He really loved me. He told me on the phone, "Paul and his mother are going shopping next week. You're going to get a ring and it's going to be gorgeous!" He was so ecstatic.

The next day I broke up with the other guy.

Later that week, Paul gave me an engagement ring. It was September, 1959.

We planned on getting married in June and were looking around to buy a house. Paul had been working with his father ever since he was a student at New York University, where he attended at night while working during the day. He had some money saved, so we decided to look on Long Island. Paul's father made plans for us to go to Paris to meet his family, but we found out that Paul couldn't go because he would be subject to the French army. We were just busy making plans and looking for a house. This was in September, October.

The roses came back. Once we were engaged, I was working and every Friday night he would meet me and bring me one rose.

One time, Paul and his father got in a fight, so Paul slept in my house. He didn't go home all week. He didn't want to talk about it. I knew he had a fight with his father, but that's all I knew. One day, his mother called to say that his father was sick. Paul went home. I saw him the next day. I only knew his father was sick, but Paul didn't tell me with what or how sick. We stopped making plans. We stopped looking for homes. We didn't make a definite plan for the wedding. This was in October or November. In January, he asked me if I would get married at his father's bedside.

I said, "Of course."

That's when he told me his father had leukemia and was dying.

When he asked me to get married at his father's bedside, I said I would. But before we could even make plans or do it, his father died. Paul took it very, very badly. We didn't make plans to get married. Sometime in March, we finally decided to have a wedding. My mother was making the wedding. She said we'd do something small at my sister's home. Paul said okay. I had the invitations made and sent out. His mother had given me a list. Every day, she and Paul would give me more and more people. From a small little wedding, they kept adding more and more names. When the invitations went out, Paul was out of town on a business trip. He called up and said, "Cancel the wedding. It's off."

"Cancel the wedding? It's off? What are you talking about?"

"Well, it's just not going to work."

I said, "Okay, what happened?"

"I'll talk to you when I get home," he said. "The wedding is off."

Of course, I was hysterical. What was going on? I think my mother's sister, with whom we were living, called him back on the phone and asked what was going on.

Mrs. David Newman
requests the honour of your presence
at the marriage of her daughter

Linda Arlene

to

Mr. Paul Robert Wattenberg

Sunday afternoon, the twenty-sixth of June
Nineteen hundred and sixty
at one o'clock

Congregation Beth Sholom
Broadway at Washington Avenue
Lawrence, Long Island

Wedding invitation.

He said, "Well, Linda and Toby (my mother) didn't put my mother's name on the invitation."

She said, "Paul, when an invitation goes out, it says, '*Mrs. Newman requests the honor of your presence...*' "

In Emily Post, it's always the girl's parents who are on the top of the invitation, but she wanted her name on top. '*Mrs. Newman and Mrs. Rae Wattenberg request...*' Well, my mother thought that her request was inappropriate. My mother and my aunt didn't understand it, but my mother said, "You know what? If that's what she wants, we'll re-send her invitations." Only hers, to her friends.

My mother had invitations reprinted, saying, '*Mrs. Toby Newman and Mrs. Rae Wattenberg request...*' and, before we knew it, another 20 people were added to the list. They kept being added and added.

We got married on June 26, 1960. The day of the wedding, we were at the synagogue in Lawrence, Long Island. I was there with my whole family, along with Paul's guests. A half-hour went by and Paul was not there. Forty-five minutes, Paul wasn't there. I was dying. Totally dying. In the end, he was an hour late to his own wedding. He was scared. His family came late with him. It was only his mother and his brother, after all.

In the Jewish religion, there is a prayer for the dead. His mother wanted this prayer recited before the wedding ceremony because her husband had just died. She wanted it done privately in a separate room. We were in a room, reciting this prayer for the dead. Not only had Paul's father recently died, but my father had died just three years before. My mother-in-law was hysterical crying, and my mother also began to weep. It was the saddest, saddest wedding anybody could ever imagine. Everybody's eyes were full of water, crying.

It was a sad day, but also a joyous one.

Linda at wedding, June 26, 1960.

Linda and Paul at Marcia's house.

Paul's brother Gary, Linda, Paul and his mother Rachel.

Linda and Paul at Marcia's home.

After the wedding, we went to my sister's house for the reception. It had to be 100°. There were many more guests than we had expected because Paul and his mother kept adding more and more people to the list.

For our honeymoon, we went into New York City and stayed at the Alrai Hotel, which is now the Plaza Athenee. We went into the city because Paul had to go to work on Monday. We checked in, went up to the room and had a bottle of champagne. It was very hot. Paul said, "I'm going to go downstairs to get a newspaper, and I'll be back in five or ten minutes."

Half an hour later, he wasn't back. I was looking out the window and saw a crowd. I figured Paul was dead! I was watching the crowd and another 15 minutes passed. Forty-five minutes went by and he still wasn't there. All of a sudden, in the crowd, I spotted him! I guess he saw me, too, and came upstairs.

I said, "What's going on?"

Elizabeth Taylor, Eddie Fisher, Natalie Wood and Robert Wagner had come in and were staying at the Alrai. They were having a party downstairs for Elizabeth Taylor. He went over to the hotel manager and said, "I'm a newlywed. We just got married this afternoon. Can we go to the party?"

He ran upstairs and told me this story (of course, after the 45 minutes that he hung around downstairs!). After this entire day, which was a nightmare of a wedding, he now told me, "Get dressed. We're going to go to Elizabeth Taylor and Eddie Fisher's party."

We went down and met them. They offered us drinks. I drank, but Paul is not too much of a drinker, so he didn't indulge. Robert Wagner kept offering me drinks. I didn't know what I was doing. I just kept drinking champagne. We came upstairs about 2:30 in the morning. I was completely drunk and spent the rest of the night in the toilet, throwing up.

So that was my wedding day and honeymoon night, spent in the bathroom throwing up.

The next morning, Paul went to work. I think we only stayed at the hotel for two nights. We rented this little apartment in Long Beach, instead. It was not like a regular apartment; it was more like a summer rental, a typical beach house. Just as we were about to go out there, Paul said, "Oh, I forgot to tell you. My brother is coming out with us."

That was the fourth night of my so-called honeymoon, which, by the way, was supposed to be in Europe! I now had a 17-year-old boy coming out to the beach to live with us. There was a young married couple with an infant child who lived around the corner. One day, they got into a big fight and the guy, who was a friend of Paul's, came up to our apartment and said, "Paul, I'm leaving my wife. I'm going down to Florida. You want to come with me?"

Paul turned to him and said, "I can't come. I'm not even married a month! How am I going to go?"

I overheard. I said, "Not even married a month? We also don't have an apartment to go to after this rental is over!"

Of course, Paul didn't go away with him. But these were the kind of crazy things that were always happening.

We decided to take an apartment in Forest Hills. My mother lived in Brooklyn and his mother lived in the Bronx, so we would be right in the middle. I had stopped working, but Paul was always after me, "Go back to work. Go back to work. Why aren't you working? Go back to work."

"Okay, I'll look for a job." Meanwhile, I was collecting unemployment, which at that time was for a month or two. But I didn't really want to go back. Paul was 30 years old. I felt I had to have children quickly. So I said what I really felt, which was, *We have to have a child immediately.*

I became pregnant two months later.

We were always kidding about the fact that Paul liked blond women. I had jet black hair. While he was at work one day, I went to the beauty salon and told the beautician, "I want to be a blond."

My hair was so dark that it wouldn't turn blond, no matter what they did. It turned a kind of fire-engine red. We lived in a place called "Parker City" in Forest Hills. When Paul came home that evening, he opened the door to our apartment and saw a redhead. He had no idea what happened and he walked out. He looked at the door, saw he was in the right apartment, and walked back in. I got hysterical. "I tried to become a blond. I couldn't. It's awful!"

He said, "Don't worry. You'll go and you'll put it back."

I woke up in the middle of the night, saw myself in the mirror and got hysterical again. This was me. Paul called my mother and my aunt. It was always the two of them because they lived together. They kept saying, "Don't worry. We'll be there tomorrow morning. We'll get the beautician to come. She'll do it in the house. You won't even have to go to the beauty salon."

So that was one catastrophe.

Paul still couldn't accept that he was married. All of a sudden, I was getting phone calls from a woman asking, "Is this Paul Wattenberg's residence?"

"Yes."

"Oh, I'm so-and-so from Detroit. I'm in for the weekend. Can I talk to him?"

I said, "You can, but he's married. And his wife is pregnant."

She hung up. He had no idea who it was. This was Paul.

I gave birth to our son, Lee, on November 15, 1961. I wasn't working. I took care of Lee. Paul was a workaholic. He would go into work in the morning and come home at 8:00 or 9:00 at night when Lee was asleep. He would wake Lee up to play with him. This would cause huge arguments because I had just spent two hours trying to put Lee to sleep.

I became pregnant again soon after and Debbie was born on January 25, 1963. When Debbie was born, I became very ill. I had a pulmonary embolism, which was a blood clot to my lung. I was hospitalized for over a month. Paul would bring Lee to see me and Lee didn't know who I was. When he came to the hospital, Paul would say, "There's Mommy!" and Lee wouldn't move. Sometimes he went to another person.

I said, "That's it. I am going to be with my children for the rest of my life and they will never forget me."

There was no way I was going to go back to work. Children were my life. I was around them all the time. But Paul always worked late. He was a very hard worker, making money, and things were financially good.

Paul even worked on Saturdays in those years. After working six days a week, he was so tired on Sundays that he couldn't lift his head off the bed. So he was never with the kids. My mother had moved from Brooklyn to Forest Hills, right across the street, and she was usually with me and the children.

Wendy was born on December 3, 1965. We decided to buy a house. Even though our apartment was gorgeous, I had wanted a house the whole time. After all, I was married, I had three children, a dog, it was the perfect picture – I wanted a house with a picket fence! That's exactly what I thought.

I went out and found a house in Great Neck, which was fairly close to New York City. Paul would be able to drive to work every day because it was only about 20 minutes farther from where we were already living. We bought the house. We still live there.

We needed to buy the house in 24 hours because, otherwise, he would have had to sign a new lease for the apartment and Paul was all about money. He never wanted to spend money. He was always saving.

When Paul started traveling for work, I went with him. But as the children got older, they said, "We don't care if Daddy goes away as long as you are home, and we don't care if you go away as long as Daddy is home."

When we realized that, we couldn't do it anymore. I stopped traveling. Lee was going to be 13 and was preparing for his Bar Mitzvah at the Plaza Hotel. Lee's Bar Mitzvah was going to be the biggest, best party we had ever given. As far as I was concerned, this was going to be the Bar Mitzvah and the wedding that I never had. Another catastrophe happened. Paul's business wasn't doing well. I suggested that we call off the Bar Mitzvah.

Paul said, "No way. I am making this Bar Mitzvah."

That wasn't like Paul, because he was usually very conservative. He was depressed, business was bad. We were crazy: how were we going to manage this? But we had the Bar Mitzvah and it was exquisite. We had the best time. He pulled out of his financial problems and all the bills were paid.

Life goes in cycles, whether it's with Paul or it's the industry or the business. You have good times and you have bad times. It's fun at the good times and it's not so much fun at the bad times. Paul's emotional. It's not easy. It's difficult. I had lived through good and bad times as a child. I knew what it was like to have everything and then lose it when my father died. I went from private schools, college, clothes, to suddenly no more schools, no more college, no more clothes. I had to go out and make a living and take on my mother as a responsibility. I worried about her and took care of her, financially, just as Paul took care of his mother. They were always our problem.

We always took care of our families. My sister Marcia and I were extremely close, even though we were totally different people. When she got divorced, Paul realized that he had to help her out. He financially helped my sister, my mother and his mother.

When our daughters got married, he made up his mind – we never really discussed it – that the time he didn't put into his own children, he was going to put into his grandchildren. He is at every single game they play, or at least a good 75% of them. He loves being with them and talks to them as a friend. He is mesmerized by his family: his children, his grandchildren. But he is still obsessed with work. He is a workaholic. He doesn't realize it when he sometimes neglects a family function or one of the children, but he has gotten better over the years. And I'm always there to remind him.

What has made this marriage a success? It's funny. We're opposites. We're also stubborn, opinionated, strong-willed. But what has made it truly work is family. When you see photographs of our grandchildren and you see our children, you know what makes us work. Family, pure and simple. This is what has made our marriage. We love to be with our family. We try to go away as a family every year, all of us together, and then I try to take the children alone.

We do fun things. I remember the time Paul got on a Segway. We do things that most of our friends won't.

Our marriage is about family, family, and friends. Both are very important to us. Family first, and then friends. As I have gotten older, I have lost some very close friends. It's been hard. I lost my mom, my sister, and my closest friend, all within a two year period. You realize that your children are important, watching them grow, enjoying their lives. But your children grow up and leave and have their own lives. As you get older, you learn to accept it.

I have learned in life: you can sometimes break rules, forgive quickly, love truly and never forget anything that makes you smile.

I look forward to seeing what life brings each day. It's good as long as you have your health, because things can change at any time. Enjoy the moments that you are given. ✱

Linda, Marcia and Toby at
Debbie's wedding, 1986.

Toby, Marcia and Aunt Sylvia, c. 1995.

Linda, Toby and Marcia at Paul and Linda's
25th Anniversary party, 1985.

Linda and Marcia, c. 1990.

Center: Marcia. Sons Steven, Mark and David and daughter, Abbey. Beth and Mitch.

l to r: Aunt Sylvia, mother Toby, Marcia, Anita, Beth, Debbie, Abbey, Linda. Seated: Wendy.
Wendy's wedding, October 1990.

Letter to Linda From her Daughters Debbie and Wendy,
and her Daughter-in-Law Laura, on her 70th birthday.

Mom,

I know you are probably confused about this little soiree. Why such a special party for your 60-something birthday? Are you 63, 65, 0r 67? Who knows? Between all the Botox, Restylane and all the other stuff I do on a weekly basis combined with all the lying about your age, I'm not sure any of us really knows for sure. More importantly though, none of us really care.

Growing up, you were the perfect role model. Always there for all of the important things – school activities, games, carpools and also working a career – first at Tapestry painting canvasses for needlepoint, then you owned an upscale clothing store Deux Amie, and finally craft shell boxes and antique jewelry. Always working with your friends and teaching us the importance of a career as well as motherhood. You really were the Modern Day Mother. Even now you are never too busy to do an errand for us or pick up the kids. That is, as long as you're not playing golf or bridge, shopping, having your hair done or out of the country traveling. You also are the professional worrier of the family. Still wondering where we are, what time we are coming home or where our kids are at all times. Not that we can blame you for all the worrying. Considering you have kids and grandchildren that play soccer and hockey, are a bit reckless and even sky dive and bungee jump.

Mom, you are always there with useful advice, and Wendy, Laura and I try to listen to you whenever we can. Why cook when you can order in? Why eat vegetables when you can eat candy? Why get presents you don't want, instead, pick them out and buy them for yourselves. Every Monday night when the housekeeper was off, we had McDonalds or Roy

Rogers. Our home was always filled with large quantities of candy and junk food. Everyone always wanted to come to our house because we didn't have a particularly strict home when it came to food. Dinner wasn't an important activity. We drank lots of soda and ate lots of candy. None of us ate vegetables until we were married. As for presents, even just this year when Daddy so desperately wanted to surprise you with your watch. The jeweler started laughing when we called him, explaining that you had just called and negotiated the entire deal.

On a more serious note, rarely do we get to tell you what a wonderful mother, friend and wife you are. We all feel so fortunate to have you in our lives. Your advice is always worthy. And you really are there for all of us 100% of the time. You have created a tight family unit with children and grandchildren that adore you. How fortunate are you to have grandchildren that would prefer to spend the entire day with you rather than be with their own parents. Whether in the toy store or clothing store you always use the grandmother's prerogative as your excuse to spoil the kids completely. You make us laugh all the time. What better way to admire your accomplishments than to look around and see this entire room filled with all of your closest friends and family. You are very special to all of us.

> Our love,
> Debbie,
> Wendy
> and Laura

6 years old, Brooklyn, 1944.

Paul and Linda, pregnant with Lee, Las Vegas, July 1, 1961.

Concorde Hotel in the Catskills, 1963.

Paul's 39th birthday surprise party.
Great Neck, NY. 1970.

Acapulco discotheque, 1978.

Capri, Italy, 1978.

Roman holiday, July 1979.

Argentina, 1982.

Sea Goddess cruise – Rome to St. Tropez, 1985.

Great Wall of China, October 16, 1998.

Standing with 1971 Mercedes 280 SE, sold in 2008, after being in the family for 37 years.

Xian, China, 1998.

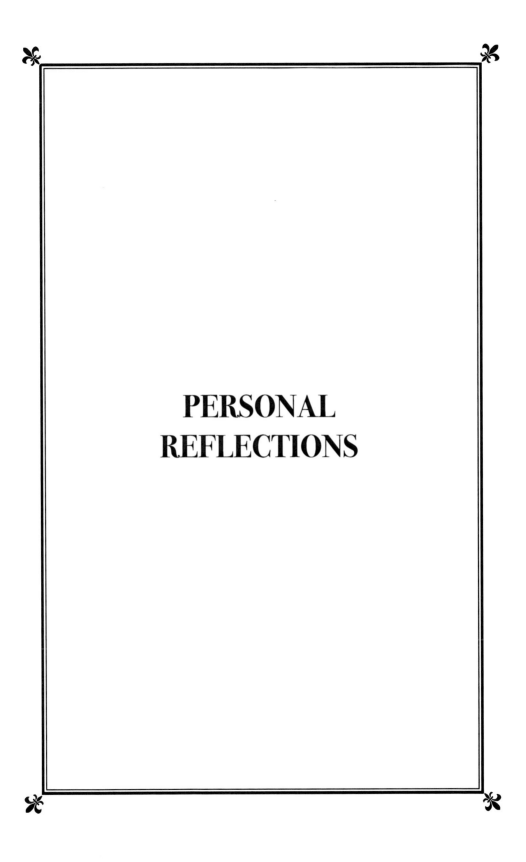

PERSONAL
REFLECTIONS

Values

Family is what it's all about, no question whatsoever. Family: your children, your grandchildren, your wife. The values of a family are something that can be considered eternal. My grandfather had the opportunity to leave Europe with us, but he wouldn't take it because his family was in Poland. He felt like it would be a betrayal of them to leave and go to America. He didn't want to do it. They eventually died and he, too, perished.

I would describe myself, as regards family, as beyond reality. There isn't anything I wouldn't do for them. I'm terribly family-oriented.

I'm also very emotional about memories. Reliving my stories has made me realize how fortunate I am that my mother had the will and courage to do what she did. It was all her doing that we escaped. I was only nine years old.

After my father died and I was going with Linda, I was nervous about getting married. I don't know if everyone feels that way. I was used to being carefree, living life as a bachelor. Confronting new, heavier responsibilities was a little scary. I may have imagined more responsibility than was realistic. Of course, as I look back now, getting married was a wonderful moment. The last 50 years have resulted in some very nice dividends, which wouldn't have happened if I hadn't taken that chance.

I have that photograph of my family, all of us sitting around. It's very special. There are moments when I'm a little nervous or a little down, and I take that picture out and look at it. It makes me feel better. That picture, that family, would never have existed if Linda and I hadn't gotten married and made a life out of it. When I really look back, I realize that Linda was very instrumental in laying the groundwork for so many things I recall with pleasure. Living with me was not an easy task.

Life has not always been lollipops and roses. Things don't always work out just the way you think they will. It's not that simple. In marriage, there are always bumps in the road, and we certainly had our share of bumps. One mistake I made in my zest to build a career was that I did not maintain the proper balance between family and business. Like many professionals, I became so pre-occupied with my career goals that I neglected the things I love the most. I neglected my family. I made sacrifices that were painful to my wife and kids. I did not spend as much time with my children as I should have. I was either traveling, trying to make sales, or trying to promote the business, devoting more time to work than I really should have. That's one regret I have. If I were to do it again, I would somehow make it my business to be there more frequently, because no matter how I look at it, the sacrifices I made while building my so-called career may not have actually advanced me that much more than if I hadn't neglected my family.

I particularly regret not having dinner with my children as frequently as possible. One of Linda's big complaints was that I was not always there for dinner with the family. I've noticed that my children, who are now grown, are home every night having dinner with their children, so I think they felt I was not there and they learned from it. They've done something that I did not do as diligently as I should have. I did have dinners with them, of course, but it was usually on the weekend.

It was important to keep striving to be successful, to provide the things I wanted them to have to be able to lead a privileged life. But loving one's family and keeping a balance between work and family are extremely important. My obsession with career wasn't really appropriate – I can see that now. What I did, I cannot undo. I try to make amends for it. I think I improved as we went along, especially over the last 20 years. Whereas I made a point to try to come to my children's sporting events, I see the extent to which they participate in their own children's sports and activities, and I realize that I did not participate with nearly the amount of devotion or time that they do. Today, with my grandchildren, I do not miss a beat. I'm there for everything. Whether it's a soccer game or hockey or basketball or lacrosse, I'm there. I'm trying to make up for lost time. It's a step toward realizing that life is not all about career and money. It's hard. I'm still ambitious, but I'm getting a little more balanced.

At the end of the day, despite all the bumps, I look back at my decision to get married and I realize it was the best decision of my life. Linda has been a very big anchor in my life. She's very special. A lot of things that we've attained, never would have occurred if she weren't there to push me along. I have a conservative nature, but no matter what it was, Linda was always there, pushing. Many of the things that we have and that we've attained are because of her tenacity. She was very, very instrumental in building our family and our life.

Enjoying family, our grandchildren and our children, is very special to me. All the hesitations that occurred before we got married, dissipated.

Of course, the other side of the coin of loving your family is losing your family. As far as sad events in life, the death of my father was very devastating. He was so young, and it is especially painful to me that he never got to see his grandchildren. My mother's dying was also devastating. I'm sure Linda went through the same thing with her father. When her sister Marcia died, that had a very emotional impact because we were there. Of course, Linda was also very close with her mother and her Aunt Sylvia. They were more than just mother and daughter or just aunt and niece. They were truly family, in the very deepest sense of the word.

I think my family knows how much I love them. They all know I'm there for them. I always will be there and, one day when I am not here, I will be with them in spirit.

Integrity and honesty are crucial traits. My children all have them.

What drove me? I think that if I were to ever fall behind, for my personality, that would be a difficult step to take. In other words, when you're in business or a career, it's great when everything falls right into place and is working out fantastically. But if you have a major financial setback, that's going backwards. Say you're living in three or four homes and suddenly you end up in one home, or maybe you're driving a nice car and now you're not driving that car. I have a certain fear of failing. The opposite of the fear of failing is the obsession to succeed. They are two sides of the same coin.

The idea of failing becomes the catalyst that drives you. This may be at the heart of the workaholic. Living and breathing, everything you are doing, seems to be interconnected with your career. There are times when that describes me. But in my inner self, I don't like it. I don't like the constant pressure, the constant reminder that I have to push forward. Wouldn't it be nice to just not do anything? That's retirement.

I think when you're younger, you're able to cope with the pressures and the bumps in the road better than when you get older. You handle it better.

In Retrospect

Did my past experiences help create the person I am today?

I think your background, and your parents' backgrounds, are very important. When I look back, I see that my father's family was very poor, but they had a rich home intellectually and spiritually. They were very Orthodox, praying to God and studying the Torah, so they felt very enriched. I understand it intellectually, but I don't comprehend it emotionally. It's not me.

Coming from such a poor family, my father left and struck out on his own at 16 or 17 years old. I can understand that. He had to be very courageous to leave home and seek adventure in the world. I think I got a lot of those traits from him. He was always in there, battling to reach his goal, whatever it was. He came from no money. Everything he did, he built up himself. It wasn't like he inherited. There's a difference between inheriting and building something yourself. You end up with a different modus operandi. If you inherit one hundred, two hundred million, I imagine it gives you a certain shield. But it's not just the money. What does it do to you emotionally? What does it do to happiness, love, and everything else?

Money in itself isn't going to make you happy. Every time one of my kids was born, it was a very, very exciting moment. Those were moments of true happiness.

What happened during the war may have scarred my emotional traits. In other words, when my father had built a little success story and the Germans came in and took everything away, we lost everything we had in France. I'm not sure if that influenced my modus operandi. It may have, but I don't know. I saw my father struggle, trying to start his life all over again when he came here. When we finally got here, it was a battle. It's an interesting question: what drives one to be obsessive in certain ways? I don't really know the answer.

My mother had a different drive. She was obsessive when she had to escape, but she was not so obsessive when it came to career. It was not the end of the world to her, which it really isn't. It took me a long time to learn that. All the perceived anxieties are something you make up in your own mind. The unknown can be bent out of shape. If there is something you don't know about, you can read into it either something positive or something negative. It can be interpreted in two different ways. For instance, there was a time when business got very difficult, when there was a transition from the domestic market to the import market. We took a substantial loss during this time. When you go through this type of transition, you have some fears of going out of business. It's natural. Ultimately, we were able to weather the storm, go through the difficult period and end up on our feet. But it took a lot of courage. A lot of people in the same situation might have just folded.

I have always felt that, in most cases, you can figure out a solution to your problems. I'm generally an optimist. In fact, I think I'm very optimistic. Even when I may not feel optimistic, I'm still optimistic. I mean that when you have some negative things happening to you, there are two ways to look at it. You can just give up, or you can think of some positive things to create from the negativity. There's always a positive. You just need to think in that way.

Those first ten years of my life have been buried in my mind. It's pushed back. I don't linger with it. It was a period of life that, fortunately, I survived and now I'm here. We were not like people who ended up in Auschwitz. They really suffered. We were on the perimeter, but we never suffered like they did. We were very fortunate in that way. It didn't leave the scars, even though I lived with my grandfather the last couple of months in Paris and he ended up in Auschwitz in the gas chambers. That's a painful, emotional trip, but it was 69 years ago. Time is a healer. One doesn't stay and belabor the point. I don't think I was as scarred as some people I know who actually lived through the camps. They went to the edge of death, and survived. It's different. My mother and I lived on the edge but, fortunately, not inside the edge. I speak to people who were in these camps. If they were in decent health, they became the body brigade. They were forced to take the dead out of the gas chambers and line them up for the ovens. That, I never experienced.

For a long time, I didn't think I was a Holocaust survivor because I had only been deprived of the emotional elements for about two years. I felt I was very fortunate. My mother also shielded me because I was only 9 or 10 years old. She had the capability to shield me from all the stress that she was going through. We spoke about it later in life. I realized, as I got older, that we were really Holocaust survivors, even though we didn't go through the death camps. We were survivors of a despicable era.

I think my experience in the Holocaust sets me apart somewhat because I think that a typical American boy or girl who was born at the same time as I was would have been too young to understand the world with Hitler. Probably they were brought up, went to public school, junior high and high school, lived in Brooklyn or the Bronx, and that was basically the highlight. What did they do? Maybe in the summertime, they'd go to camp in the Catskills. Maybe they'd go to Long Beach for a month or two in the summer. Maybe their parents were struggling to get by.

The story of my experience in the Holocaust is something I want people to know and remember. This president of Iran, who denied that the Holocaust ever happened, is an insult to our intelligence. He had a whole group of people research the topic, to see if the whole event ever occurred. This is an insult. It has been scrupulously documented. When there is such hatred with these radical Islamic people, it's unreasonable.

I feel that a Holocaust could happen again. I feel that the whole world is being confronted with a potential repeat performance, like a Hitler, but in a much greater magnitude. You had maybe eighty million people in Germany against the world. Now you have a billion Moslems, if they all were to unite. (Thank God that the majority of Moslems are moderate.) There's a fortunate and unfortunate side to it. Look at Iraq. You have the Shi'ites and the Sunnis. They're killing each other. In Palestine, you have *Hamas* and you have *al Fatah*. This week, they killed each other again. So everybody is against each other. But can you imagine if they all united? They'd be a very potent force. So if you ask, *Could it happen again?* I answer yes, but with qualifications. Meaning, we live in uncertain times, but we live in times of great communication. If any one group or country were to do anything very foolish, it would become world information within 15 seconds. It's not as simple as it was 50 or 60 years ago when communications were more limited. But could it happen again? It's got great possibilities, as sad as that sounds.

Friendship

I have been blessed with some beautiful friendships, some that have lasted almost a lifetime. I want to mention a few people because they've been very special in my life.

I've spoken already about Shelly and Marilyn Fireman. Shelly and I have been friends for over 68 years. I am his partner in his restaurants. He's a very good listener, a very good friend and very bright. He's always been there through thick and thin, through difficult times and good times. We've had a good bond together. I feel blessed by his friendship.

I have a good friend by the name of Philip Elkus, and his wife Estelle. We've been friends probably over 50 years. He has really been more than a friend. He is always there. We spend time together. He's certainly a good listener. He's been very helpful in some financial ventures, as he's very bright and is a very successful retail merchant in Detroit. Our friend-

Shelly Fireman and me, on my 60th birthday, 1991.

Bob Katz, Murray Eisen, me, Stu Cooper, Shelly Fireman, and Sidney Myers
on my 60th birthday, 1991.

ship is full of love and understanding, as he is a fine human being and a very sensitive, caring type of guy.

I'd like to mention Stuart Cooper and his wife Sylvia. We've been friends over 40 years. Stuart is a doctor and he was always there for me. Of course, being a doctor, sometimes I would call on him, having some events, a kidney stone here or there. He was always ready to help. Medicine aside, he is a good and caring person.

I'd like to mention Murray and Roberta Eisen. We've been friends for over 55 years. That's a long, long bonding. Any events or anything that takes place, whether it's golf, fishing or boating. When I bought my boat, he was the one who encouraged me. Here I took a big boat – it was a 41-foot Criss-Craft motor yacht and I got behind the helm, which was completely illogical, but he was there to help me. So I skippered the boat

Linda, Shelly and Marilyn Fireman, and me. Tuscany, 2008.

Phillip Elkus, Linda, Estelle Elkus, and me. c. 1999.

Mexico, 1980. Bob Katz, Stu Cooper and me.

Linda, me, Sylvia and Stu Cooper, 1990.

Me and Stu Cooper, 1975.

My 39th birthday, 1970. Murray Eisen, me and Stuart Cooper.

from Lindenhurst to Capri Marina in Long Island. Roberta Eisen I met before Murray did! She was 16 years old and, unfortunately, she passed away about 14 years ago. But Murray has always been a friend and was, and is, always there for me.

Bob and Sandy Katz have been close and caring friends since way back – well, since I took Sandy to her Sweet 16 party! We spend many vacations together, having fun, and enjoying many adventurous trips throughout the world.

Sid and Judy Myers, Judy Myers in particular was my wife's best friend and her partner in *Deux Amie*. They had a bond and a friendship that went beyond friendship, throughout their lives. Each was always there for the other. Sidney has always been a friend, always been there. He's a caring type of guy.

Sandy Katz, Judy and Sid Myers, Linda, Bob Katz and me.

Back: Brenda Ashkenaz, Jessie Gottlieb, Jack Steivelman, Karen Blechman, Linda, Billy Mack, me, Phyllis Mack. Front: Howard Blechman, Susan Strauss, and Harriet Steivelman.

During the many years of living in Great Neck, we were fortunate to meet and become good friends with Susan and David Strauss, Karen and Howard Blechman, Phyllis and Bill Mack, Midge and Morty Howard, Eleanor and Norman Weiss, Joe and Barbara Dymond, Harriet and Jack Steivelman, Ronnie and Allan Gibstein, and Karen and David Fox.

As far as business people who have been very special in our lives, I'd like to mention Sam Souan, who is a good friend. He is a fine gentleman, always sincere. We have a 30 year friendship. I consider him a very special person, one who is caring and one who is a very good merchant in our apparel industry.

Bob and Sandy Katz, me and Linda, Acapulco, 1984.

The Wisdom of Experience

I've had some medical problems as I've gotten older, but I have been very fortunate in each case to live to talk about it. I had heart bypass surgery on May 20, 1990. I had prostate cancer in 2001. The anniversary of my surgery is September 5th. When you have these type of things, you develop a subconscious, psychological realization that the immortality of a human being is not, in fact, so immortal. We're all subject to termination. Those thoughts are a little scary. You realize that when these incidents occur and you are able to talk about them at some later date, you are blessed, because there are plenty of people I have known with prostate cancer who have passed away. Plenty of people with heart disease who have passed away. That has made me very conscious of physical health. I'm very measured in trying to protect my own health. When I spoke to a doctor recently, I said, "Well, how does it look? It's been eight years. Would you consider me cured?"

He said, "With cancer, I don't use the word 'cured.' Not yet."

Which means, in the back of your mind, there is the possibility of a recurrence, which would be a disaster. I no longer feel immortal. Has it changed my personality? I don't think so. Someone who has gone through these episodes might change their whole modus of life. I think, if anything, I have just gone merrily on my way, as I did prior to these illnesses. Of course, during the first year when you are going through this very jeopardized moment in your life, when you don't know whether or not you'll survive, you are concerned and scared. You wonder if you should make radical changes. Health becomes the whole focus of your life. Whether it's the heart or prostate cancer, your whole goal is to survive. This becomes a very special focus. But as you go along and things seem to be under control, either stabilized or in remission, while you do make some changes, you go back to some of your old ways.

Some people may change because they say, *Well, you're here for a short while. Might as well have fun.* I haven't had as much fun as I should. Although we've traveled all over the world and we move around a lot, I think I could do better. That's one of my wife's complaints, that we don't take enough leisure time. We have a beautiful home in Florida. We have a home in Great Neck and we have a home here in Manhattan, so we have three very nice places. But I don't take advantage of them the way I should.

I'm intense and sometimes I have a tendency to overreact to situations. I can be overly anxious. When I can step back a little, I realize, *It wasn't so terrible. No need to have that anxiety.*

You can get anxiety if you've developed a certain lifestyle and then you face some bumps in the road, which are, nevertheless, inevitable in every business. I would say I have a tendency to overreact to those bumps. This isn't good. I've gone to therapy to find out why I do that. I don't know if it's the Holocaust or something else that happened in my youth, that whenever there is some kind of an obstacle, I overreact. It's not good because when I reflect on it later, after the so-called bump has straightened out, I say, *Gee, it wasn't so bad. I overreacted.* That's not a good trait. I'm trying not to overreact when I can. I don't take it out on other people. I do it to myself. I get anxiety, I don't feel well – things of that nature.

Therapy is the best thing that ever happened. My therapist realized I was anxious and upset. I was having problems with the labor union. They were threatening to put us out of business. They wanted me to become a full union member, but I knew that would totally destroy our overhead structure. I figured it was the end of the world and I reacted accordingly. The therapist said to me, "I want to ask you something. Are you ready to die because this thing isn't going exactly the way you want?"

When he put it in that perspective, I could step back from the plate and say, *Wait a minute. I certainly don't want to die over some stupid union deal or some stupid business deal that's not working out right. Life is too valuable and too precious and much more important than that.* That's how you talk to yourself, calm yourself down.

You have to cope with the problems. At the end of the day, no matter how big the problems look or how insurmountable the obstacles appear, all those things will resolve themselves in a reasonable fashion. They won't turn out be as negative or disastrous as you anticipated or perceived them to be. The imagination runs away with itself, creating anxiety and overreaction.

When I got sick with my heart, my mother had just died. She died April 1st, 1990. Two months later, I fell ill. I think it was all interrelated. I just couldn't accept her dying. We had a huge closeness. I couldn't accept that she was gone. I was in denial. It wasn't good. I got very sick.

My rabbi came in as I was being sedated going into the operating room. I told him I was very scared that I wouldn't come out alive. He said to me, "Repeat these words. Have no fear. God is with you." I kept repeating that until they anaesthetized me and I was put out. Now 20 years later, I'm still talking about it! But it was a very emotional, scary moment.

I wrote a letter to my wife and children the day before the surgery. I gave it to my wife and told her not to open it.

I said, "If I die, I want you to open it."

That's how scared I was. I still read that letter sometimes. I wrote it while I was partially sedated, waiting for surgery. The surgery was scheduled for about 7:00 a.m. and I started writing it about midnight the night before. So I guess I'm a very emotional, anxious person.

Some anxiety can be good from the point of view of, if you see a train coming towards you, you get out of the way. But if you overreact when it's not, in fact, a train, it's not good. Something I want my children and grandchildren to realize is that, no matter what comes along, there is always a silver lining around the corner. I know this for a fact. No matter how difficult things look, they'll get better. There's no question about it. It's never as terribly disastrous as you perceive it to be at the moment because, in reality, six months later, it shall pass.

I also have a very stubborn side. I prefer to have things done my way, but I have matured enough to realize that there are other ways and, sometimes, even better ways than I first perceived. I'm not always right. That's a lesson that comes with time. It was very hard for me to change. When I worked with my father, we had our differences of opinion, young generation and old generation. He wanted things done his way and I wanted them done my way. Now my son, we have the same problem – he wants things his way and I want them mine. But now the twain meets and we compromise. Or I give in to him. I've reached a point where I don't relish the fighting that can occur with differences of opinion.

I have real drive. But at this stage of my life, I have mixed emotions. At one moment, I feel like I'm 20 years old. The next moment, I realize I'm far from 20. As you get older, there's a defense mechanism in your brain that enables you almost to act as if it's somebody else who's your age. You remove yourself from yourself, in a way. Your perspective changes. Depending on your personality, I think the human brain is equipped to avoid thinking about the end of one's life, as if it will last forever. Of course, this is a bit of a denial.

I don't know if the same is true of other people my age or older, but the thought of death, realistic as it is, is blocked out of my mind. It's a blocked-out emotion. I was just talking to a guy my age and he said, "We're blessed. You and I go back a long time. We're still here."

I said, "I want to wish you a very happy New Year and good health and here's to continuing doing this together for the next 40 years. I'm going to form a club, called 'The 119 Year-Old Club.'"

The guy was laughing. He said, "What does that mean?"

I said, "If you want to be in that club, you've got to think that you want to live to be a minimum of 119."

He said, "Count me in."

That's kind of a positive attitude. It may be totally unrealistic. They just had an article in *The New York Times*, the oldest living woman just died at 114 years old. I'm putting this guy into the 119 Year-Old Club, which I think is a rarity. But I think my head is geared up like that. I can't think differently. Realistically, it may be a fantasy. But I live in fantasy.

It would be nice, when you reach certain stages of life, to reach certain goals that you set for yourself. The alternative is to set goals so high that you are forever striving and never really get there. That could be good, too, in a way, because you don't want to set your goals too low. I think my goals are always high, insatiable, in fact. I am always trying to reach a goal which is so high that I don't feel sated at the end. I never quite fulfill it. For me, that is good. I think the zest for life comes from striving to achieve something – whether that something is defined as financial success or an emotional goal – that's within your grasp, but you are always reaching further out. I do believe that you have to set your goals high.

Of course, if you set your goals low, that may be the most pragmatic. You could say to yourself, *Well, I can only be an elevator operator*, and you become an elevator operator and you are satisfied. Maybe there are people like that. Probably there are. I always feel that, instead of being the elevator operator, I would like to own the piece of real estate the elevator is on! That's probably a sickness unto itself, that I can't be happy. The elevator operator may have a certain contentment. *Look, I'm an elevator operator. I have my pension plan. I get two days a week off, I'm happy.*

I think as a person building a career, you set your goals and you try to really achieve them, if you can. If you fall short of the goal, that's okay, too. At least you made progress.

When you set your goals high enough, if you do achieve them, you really feel a sense of accomplishment. Everything in life is very relative. My daughter just became an associate professor of dermatology at Mt. Sinai. It was a very exciting thing for her. I guess getting a professorship puts you at a different level than your peers, showing you are a little more knowledgeable, with a little more responsibility. That's a sense of accomplishment. At the end of the day, it's not all monetary. There has to be a certain amount of self-esteem and maybe some recognition from your peers. It's a nice feeling to receive peer recognition and to attain a sense of accomplishment.

I think I've achieved some recognition. I think I've reached a certain level, but because my goals are always so high, I'm still not there. The lack of contentment, in that sense, is not good. There's a juxtaposition. I like it and I really don't like it. I am always seeking the next level, maybe without the capability of feeling real contentment.

I have a goal. My goal would be that I stop working and become a person of leisure, not on the constant merry-go-round of continuous pressure. There's a certain amount that I like about it, but as I've reached this point in my life, I think I'm really ready to just glide along a little bit. I don't know if I would glide completely, but maybe I'd want to retire

65%. Still be involved 35%. I'm trying to figure out how I'm going to get to this next plateau. Maybe if I could do that and enjoy it, I would go the other 35%. I've had some friends who retired and got sick. Yet, I have some friends who retired and are having a good time.

They say, "How can you keep working? You want to be carried out with your boots on?"

What stops me from retiring? I feel a responsibility to my family, to my kids, which may just be something in my own mind. I think of being in business with my son, not wanting to leave him in the business unless it's well-solidified and everything is perfect. But there's no such thing as perfect. So I'm imagining something that probably doesn't exist. Look at Ford, an icon. It's now twelve billion dollars in debt. Chances are they could go out of business. If it happens to them, it could happen to anybody.

So I stay in to help, to assist, to try to keep that from happening. Someone might say, *If they are going to fail, let them fail on their own. It's a learning curve.* But you don't want to see anybody failing. You want everyone to be doing well. On many occasions, my son has told me to retire. Somewhere I read, *When parents get older, the children are subconsciously saying, 'When are you out of here?'* They want to do their own thing.

My wish list would be: I would love to just step back and my son would do very well, my two daughters would do very well, and I'd be here to help them with whatever they might need. It would be my pleasure. But you can't really protect the whole world. I have eight grandchildren and I want to help them, too. But as you get older, it almost gets to be impossible. It would be nice if I could set everybody up in such a way that they are emotionally and financially secure for the rest of their lives. I would have to be a multi-millionaire many times over to do that. We're not poor people, but you know. I'm going to a 70th birthday party at the Mandarin Hotel. This guy built the Mandarin. He left his kids eight hundred million dollars. That's a nice thing, but not everybody can leave eight hundred million dollars.

I am having fun, too. I work hard and I play hard. My golf game has been an obsession, but I don't play too well! I'm doing a little better lately. I could use some more vacations. And lessons! Funny story. When I went to be interviewed to join Fresh Meadows Country Club, I was into boating at the time. I had a big boat, two, as a matter of fact. This was from 1973 to 1982. My wife wanted to join a country club. She didn't really love boating. Usually, people go for these kinds of interviews, they're afraid of getting blackballed, afraid they won't gain admission, they're afraid they won't get accolades from their peers. The fear of rejection is a great fear. I went to my interview and they said, "Why do you want to join the club?"

I said, "I'll be honest with you. If you refuse me, I'll probably be very happy."

They got hysterical. I was really into boating. It wasn't the end of the world if I didn't get into the country club. But because I told them that it wasn't the end of the world if I didn't get in, they took me. I've enjoyed the last 34 years at the club. Now, of course, I'm attempting to play golf for the last 20 years – I'm still in the learning mode (*laughs*). I'm trying to hit the ball straight, but somehow I have many slices and hooks. But I haven't given up!

I believe my children are all capable. I think I've given them my best, not just financially, but emotionally and courageously. If I were to retire tomorrow, I think they would all do great. But everybody could use a little help. I think that each child has a different courageous personality.

As far as choosing a career, I believe you have to really love what you're doing to be successful in it, no matter what field you are in. If you're doing something that you don't really like, you may do well, but the chances of success are less than if you're doing something that you have a passion for. This is true whether you are in medicine, law, fashion, finance, or real estate. You have to have a passion for what you are doing. Of course, clear thinking is important, too. You have to have a head for business. But if you don't love it, you'll be very frustrated.

It's very hard to go to high school or college and predict what you are going to do. But if you have a very strong mind and a little luck, you will succeed in whatever you undertake. What would I like each grandchild to do? I think each one should do what he or she likes best. You can't influence so many people and tell them what they should do. For each person, it's a different set of circumstances. My three grandsons, Ryan, Cory and Andrew, are a hockey team. They are almost like professional hockey players. I sometimes wonder if that will be their career, if they will become professional hockey players. That's certainly far removed from the fashion business.

My daughter the doctor, Debbie, her two daughters are both extremely intelligent, they could be anything they want to be. They could be lawyers, they could be doctors, they could be entrepreneurs. My granddaughter Jamie has gotten early admission to medical school. Kyle, my grandson, is also very bright. He could be anything he wants to be. I think that applies to all of them. Education is very important.

On a recommendation level, as I said before, I like real estate, as well as financial markets and money management. I think learning about and being involved in real estate is a great opportunity. You have to have patience and staying power, because real estate runs in cycles, as I learned from my bad experience. But I was not sophisticated in that area. As I look back, I could certainly recommend it to them.

The fashion business? Let me tell you. If you think about it, you've got to really stick to your point of view and have a very determined perspective of who you want to be, where you want to be, and what you'd like to attain. There are many people in the apparel business who have made huge, huge successes. Probably the most successful one in the world right now is Ralph Lauren. He stuck to his point of view and built an empire.

What I'm really saying is, no matter what endeavor you undertake, you've got to find your particular niche and be good at it. If you have a passion for it and believe it in, you'll attain whatever goals you set for yourself.

As far as advice for my grandchildren, I have three famous words: conceive, believe, and achieve. I have always felt very optimistic about everything. Whatever you strive to accomplish in life, I believe that you first have to conceive, meaning you have to conceive an idea, a thought, or a feeling. Then you have to truly believe in it. If you conceive it and truly believe in it, your chances of achieving it are within your reach. The three words – conceive, believe, and achieve – all end the same way. I think that's my life's motto. I fully believe that if my grandchildren conceive and believe, they'll achieve. This could give them a motto, not only for business ventures, but in personal quests as well. If you conceive a family life and you believe in it, you'll achieve the ultimate of what family life is all about. The three words are intertwined.

The more you believe you will succeed, the more likely you are to succeed. If you think positively, you'll succeed. It's all perception, a self-fulfilling prophecy. One thing you can't forget is that, in life, there are successes, but there are failures, too. I think the key is: a failure is not really a failure. A failure sometimes occurs and it's really a learning experience. If you learn from that experience, you can make a comeback and try to improve on the mistakes you might have made and do better. I think that the ability to learn from mistakes is within each human being, but you have to find it within yourself and make it happen. For some people, when they get into trouble, they get into a state of depression. The idea is, instead of a state of depression, you've got to be optimistic. Think positive and you'll reach your goal. Conceive, believe, and achieve.

But you must not lose perspective. It's also very important to live life in the moment. If you focus too heavily on the attainment of your goals instead of on the process of living your life, you will find yourself living too much in the future instead of the present. You will get caught up in wanting more and more, regardless of what you may have already achieved. An excessive dependency on the results of success will increase your sense of deprivation and insufficiency, and you will not be able to enjoy the present. You find that you lose perspective, concentrating so much on the future that you lose the moment.

Live your life each day as you would climb mountains. An occasional glance towards the summit puts the goal in mind. Many beautiful scenes can be observed from each new vantage point. Climb steadily and enjoy each passing moment. The view from the summit will serve as a fitting climax to the journey.

These are philosophical thoughts to be left for the grandchildren and the great-grandchildren.

I love every one of my children and grandchildren. What I'd like to tell each one of them is that they should always think optimistically; they should always try not to be discouraged in the face of adversity. In life, there are always going to be adverse incidents, times of emotional, financial, or spiritual difficulties. Through it all, they should always know that under the cloud, there is sunshine. At the end of the day, all troubles, no matter what life throws at you, get resolved on a happy note. Of course, we're not talking about irreversible sickness. We're talking about the normal trials and tribulations of life, the human condition. Somehow, there is always a happy resolution.

I would like my grandchildren to think that way. Even if things are tough, they are going to get better. As bad as things appear at the moment, when you look back at your tough time later, you realize that it wasn't as terrible as you originally perceived it to be. I would like them to cherish that optimism, that spirit of hope. As human beings, they are much more important than even they themselves believe themselves to be. Each one of them is very special. Each one has a great career and a great future. They can all reach whatever goal they want to reach. I totally believe in them, 128%. ✶

The Family, 2008.

At the entrance to Auschwitz.
Gate has quote: "Arbeit macht frei" – "Work will make you free," July 2007.

EPILOGUE:
EXTENDED FAMILY
The Legacy
of the Holocaust

Neutrality helps the oppressor, never the victim.
Silence encourages the tormentor, never the tormented.

Elie Weisel
Nobel Laureate

After the war, the grim reality of our family's devastation emerged. We did not yet have any details, but when so few people returned, we understood. There were some survivors and some stories of incredible personal heroics, both of my family members and of those who saved them.

On my mother's side of the family, her sister, Tobi, with whom we had originally tried to escape to Spain in our car, hid out with her husband in France and survived. Her husband, my Uncle Chuna, while he survived the war, died very young, in 1950 or 1955, in Paris. My mother's brothers Abe and Hersh, who were living in France, also survived. They hid throughout the whole war. My mother's eldest sister Shendel (Sally), her husband Isaac, and their daughter Anna, who were in Poland, were able to escape by traveling east to Almata in Khasakstan. In other words, they went towards Russia and were able to survive. After the war, we got them papers and they came over to the United States. One of my mother's brothers, Isaac Bajczman, was in the concentration camp. He perished in Auschwitz. Fortunately, his wife, Loli, and his son, Georges Bajczman, hid out in the French Free Zone. They both survived.

My cousin Betty, Tobi and Chuna's daughter who was also in the car with us during our attempted escape to Spain, remembers that her family lived together in the Occupied Zone for about seven or eight months after we left, but then things got hot. Her parents decided it was best not to travel together as a family. They felt that a 10-year-old girl with a mother and father would look very obvious compared to a woman alone, a man alone, or a little girl. So they made arrangements to send Betty to the Free Zone, where they put her in a Christian home. Her parents paid the family, although the family did not want to take the money. She stayed with this Christian couple for three years, never once seeing her parents nor having any correspondence. She thought she would never see them again and was totally destroyed, emotionally. But the Christian couple were very kind people and they treated her as if she were their daughter. They used to go to church together. For that three year period, she became a Christian. Years later, they came to her wedding. In a happy ending to that story, Betty's father and mother survived the Holocaust and they were all reunited at the end of the war.

One of my mother's sisters, Eva, perished along with her husband. The story I was told was that her husband was a doctor and he supposedly kept a supply of cyanide pills. He saw the torture and other horrific acts the Germans were committing, especially upon the women. When he and my aunt were captured, they decided it was better to commit suicide. I cannot verify that this story is true, but that is what I heard.

On my father's side of the family, his brother Joseph had been a prisoner-of-war. He survived and returned to Paris. His other brother, Morris, also survived, having escaped from Camp Gurs and gone into hiding. He just died a few years ago at the age of 89.

In 1955, my mother, father and brother went to Paris as a Bar Mitzvah present for my brother. They went on *The Queen Mary*, which at that time was considered a luxury liner. I was already 24 or 25 and I had to stay in New York to watch my father's business. My father hadn't been back to Europe since August, 1939. It was during this trip that he found out the devastating news of how so many people in the family were killed. We "knew" what had happened, of course, when so few of his family came back in 1946, but this is when he learned the grisly details.

His family was decimated.

His mother, father, five sisters and one brother, Avrum, who was not much older than me, were all killed by the Germans. Some were in Auschwitz, others were machine-gunned right in their hometown.

It was very traumatic for my father to wake up one day and know, beyond a shadow of a doubt, that his whole family was gone.

My dad's brother, Morris, of course, also learned about the brutal demise of his entire family. I didn't realize until I was much older the emotional impact it had on him. I was on a visit to Paris in the late 1990s, and I asked him about temple. He said, "My mother, my father, my sisters, brothers, all killed by the Germans. You want me to believe in God?" He would no longer even go to temple. He lost faith completely. That shocked me. They were such an ultra-Orthodox family.

My father's sister, Rachel, who had come to Paris to help my grandfather because she could cook kosher, she married Léon Groner on May 15, 1941. France was occupied by the Nazis at that point. They were both deported to Auschwitz in July, 1942 on convoy number six.

During the trip to Paris in 1955, my father heard a story about his father, Isaac. Although I don't know the exact details, my cousin Frida Wattenberg told me that my grandfather was arrested. They had a round-up camp in Paris called *Ile d'Hiver*, which means Winter Garden, which is where they rounded up all the Jews. My grandfather realized that being arrested, rounded up, and taken away was not good.

Before he left, my grandfather entrusted his gold pocket watch to the superintendent of his building. This man was a friend of his. He said to the super, "Look, I have one grandchild and his name is Paul. When we come back, or when any of my kids come back, make sure that Paul gets this particular watch."

Aunt Rachel (Rougea) and Leon Groner, married May 15, 1941.

When my father went to Paris in 1955, this superintendent, who was a very honest man, gave the watch to him. Nobody would have known the difference if he had not — that's the type of person he was.

Some of my father's cousins survived. My cousin Frida wrote a book about her experiences in the war, which she spent working with the French Resistance. She was responsible for saving the lives of about 1000 Jewish children who were smuggled into Switzerland. She also helped some members of our family to survive. At great risk to herself, she took all kinds of chances and persevered. She has dedicated her entire life to the memory of all the people who were killed, so that the world should never forget what truly happened.

Frida has a little story about my grandfather, which I'll translate from the French. Basically, she says:

> I believe your grandfather, Isaac Wattenberg, had a cardiac problem and he was hospitalized from all the stress and problems that came with being arrested. I do recall that I went to see Professor Soulis, one of the great cardiologists of the era, and asked him if, because of your grandfather's illness, could he be released. It served absolutely nothing. It fell on deaf ears. I continually asked if he arrived at Auschwitz, the death camp, after he left. Your grandfather left his gold pocket watch for you and he left his gold pen for the forthcoming grandchild, who did not yet have a name. Your cousin, Jackie, had not yet been born, as your Aunt Ida was pregnant in Camp Gurs.

This is very emotional for me. I only heard this story recently. I never really knew what happened.

The Germans kept such meticulous records. I have here a document regarding my grandfather: *Yankel Wattenberg, born 1885 in Brzinicy, Poland. Deported from Drancy.* Drancy was the round-up camp outside of Paris. They took him to Auschwitz and they wrote down the convoy number, 33. The date was September 16th, 1942. He was gassed and cremated.

There is a book that records about 20,000 or 50,000 kids from Paris that disappeared. I have the book. In that book, they have pictures of my cousins and what cattle car they were in and the exact date they were deported to Auschwitz. The Germans kept exact records, as if human beings were inventory. My cousin, Jackie Bajczman, and his mother were arrested. He didn't want to be separated from his sister, Jacqueline, so the Germans said, "Okay, you can come together." So they took the mother, who was my aunt, my cousin who was two years older than me, and his little baby sister who was two years younger than me. They took the three of them in a cattle car. They were gassed and killed in Auschwitz.

The process was strictly methodical, totally inhumane.

When my father went to Europe, he tried to recover some of the assets we had left. The German government recognized claims for suffering during the Holocaust, and my father's two brothers, Joseph and Morris, were being paid reparations. But one had been a prisoner-of-war and the other went through the whole episode. My father figured they had suffered enough, so he didn't pursue it. We had actual legitimate claims, but at that time, there was still a lot of denial. Much of what had happened was not yet being acknowledged by the Germans.

What I reflect in my mind is that we had such a huge family. A big part of the family was in Poland, although we also had segments that had migrated to Paris. They were all my cousins: girl cousins, boy cousins. I remember from the time I was born, playing with them and having fun. Just like when you see all my little grandchildren, when they all get together, they're having the best time. My mother was the sixth in a family of seven children. Her older brothers and sisters, a lot of them had children, all of whom were my first cousins. When we used to get together on Saturdays and Sundays, they would come to our house or we would go to theirs. I recall all those kids.

On my father's side, none of his brothers or sisters were married because my father was the eldest. His brother didn't get married until 1939 and he didn't have any children until 1941 or 1942, after we left for America. On my father's side, I was the only grandchild anyone ever knew. But I got to know everyone and was doted upon. So it's strange to me that anybody who became part of the family in America, for them it's like the European part of the family never existed.

"Yeah, they were in Auschwitz. They all died."

The old family didn't exist, as far as the new kids.

Visiting Auschwitz/Birkenau

What I must say is that for a great part of this book, I was really ob-sessed and focused on Auschwitz and the Holocaust and the audacity of the Iran President's recent statements that the Holocaust never occurred. I had an empty feeling: how could I talk about the Holocaust without ever hav-ing been to Auschwitz and Birkenau? So in September, 2007, my wife Linda and I made a special trip and we went to Prague. We saw the devas-tation that occurred there with the Jewish men, women and children. Then we went to the ultimate disaster area which is called Auschwitz and Birke-nau. The guide that we had was a Polish man who was extremely sympa-thetic and asked me, *After all these years, why did I come now to Auschwitz?*

I told him I was writing a book and I had a very strong urge to feel the land, walk in the footsteps and breathe the air where most of my fam-ily perished. It was a very strange feeling, I still can't really figure it out. So we went there and the guy took us to the gas chambers, which are now set up as a museum. You can actually see how the people were gasp-ing for air and scraping the walls in a desperate attempt to get air. They made it like showerheads. They gave everybody soap and people thought they were going in for a shower. They ended up being gassed. This was a trip and a half, very emotional. The guide said to me, "Being that you are from France, would you like me to take you to the actual buildings where the French Jews were kept?"

You see, when they came, they kept them together in one envi-ronment. They took a building that should have had maybe 50 people and they put in 300 people. There were very poor toilet facilities, no showers. They were being treated like sub-human beings. I went through that whole episode and he said to me, "Why don't I take you to the French display?"

I said, "What is that?"

He said, "Well, there is a hall where they show you all the photographs of people from France who were killed in Auschwitz."

So I went there immediately because I was looking for my grandfather, Isaac Wattenberg. I couldn't find him. There were thousands of pictures. But as I was walking along, I found two photographs of my cousin Jackie Bajczman, who was my mother's brother's son, and his little baby sister. He was 11 at the time when he was gassed, and she was seven. So it was a realistic wake-up and sort of a confirmation that there's no doubt of what happened. This again reflects on these people in Iran and some people in the Islamic society. The fair-minded ones know the Holocaust occurred. But some of them, like the President of Iran and some of his sidekicks, have stated that it never happened. These are things that took place.

Having been there, now I can speak about it. Before I was speaking about what I heard from others or what I saw in the cinema or on television. In this case, I actually wanted to be there. I feel more closure. Auschwitz was a reality where millions of innocent men, women and children perished. ✶

Letter (email) from Cousin Jacques Wattenberg
August 12, 2008

Subject: Mishpohe's (Family's) Fate

What we know for sure:
Grandpa Icek and Aunt Rougea passed away in the *lager* (Auschwitz death camp). Same about Aunt Rougea's husband.

What I heard (don't remember from whom exactly): Aunt Anna passed away before the war or during the war, but not directly killed by the Germans (why is unclear: disease?).

What we don't know is the fate of Grandma Shaindel, her daughters our Aunts Feïga (the blonde one), Frida (the younger one), and her son, Uncle Avraham.

We know, however, that the vast majority of the remaining Jews in Tomaszow's ghetto (including Jews brought in from other locations) were gathered in the Jewish cemetery to be machine-gunned to death. Two mass graves are in existence right in front of the main entrance of the cemetery.

Our grandparents' house was located on the inside brim of the ghetto, at the junction of the two ghettos' areas. Today, it is a public garden. May G. avenge their blood.

In other towns of the Lodzkie area which I visited, the municipalities have displayed signs, posters, plaques to remember the Jewish citizens who used to live, toil, and thrive here. There is nothing in Tomaszow except inside the cemetery, which is in a remote section of the town (*uber die bruck*) on the Warshaw road.

All best wishes *und Zeï gezint.* ✶

*Letter from Frida Wattenberg (translated from French),
written in Paris on July 31, 2006*

My Dearest Paul,

I have just finished the parcel that I am sending you. It is neither literature nor style, but I have tried to remember bit by bit the memories in order to give you the information that you need for your book of memoirs which you want to pass on to your children and your grandchildren.

I remember hearing my parents tell (I must have been very young as they separated when I was only 6) that your father Leon Wattenberg had arrived in France as a tourist on the Côte d'Azur, and when he arrived in Paris at the train station it was cold and my father lent him his coat, because he had arrived from Palestine in "tourist clothes of the Côte d'Azur." Have you heard this story?

Later, for a reason unknown to me, my mother, who had a difficult character, did not go to Boulevard Magenta anymore. I still went, and your mother used to come to our home, 13 rue des Ecouffes, especially when she came to shop on rue des Rosiers. We always had very good relationships with your Uncles Maurice and Joseph.

I remember very well the arrival of your grandfather and Rougea in Paris. At the reunion that we see in the photo, you cannot see me, but I was there. I will tell you about my first encounter with my uncle, your grandfather. I was 12 or 13 years old and I was already going to the Lycée Victor Hugo. He took me aside – I speak Yiddish – and he asked me if my family was ruined for putting all these good things on the table. I remember answering him that on rue des Rosiers you could buy 3 bananas for one franc. It's true that poor vendors would sell lemons and bananas in bunches of three in the street. It →

is odd that I am not in the photo, but I quite remember being there. I also do not see my mother or my Uncle Aaron's family in the photo.

Rougea learned quickly how to get to rue des Ecouffes from rue de Lancry and Mama showed her where to shop at the kosher stores that were not too expensive. I remember helping her after school on Friday afternoons with her Shabbat shopping bags.

Your grandfather was a formidable type. One day he said to me, "You want to earn a little money?" As I said yes, he asked me to teach him French. He bought at the temple's library (which still exists today on rue de Rosiers) a special book and I started to give him French lessons.

The political climate was beginning to worsen and your grandfather worried terribly for his wife and children who had stayed behind in Poland. There was a lesser worry in the family, as your Uncle Maurice wanted to get married "with a Turk," Aida. At those times it was rare. Do the Ashkenazis and Sephardics recognize themselves?

I remember the "schtibel" (temple) rue Dieu, where our parents went to pray. I see it well. Zizi, Maurice and I, the children, it made us laugh.

Then there was the general mobilization. The family all left by car towards Villers on the Sea, where Maurice and Aida had just been on vacation. We immediately reserved a place there to insure our protection in case Paris was bombed on September 1st, 1939!! I remember when we arrived near the ocean, your grandfather exclaimed, "*A yam mit wasser* (a sea with water)" and this made us all laugh. I think at that time your father was in New York where he had gone for the World's Fair.

A few days later we returned to Paris and my mother sent me to boarding school at the Lycée de Poitiers so that I →

could study in peace. I returned to Paris after the defeat. Bernard and his brother Maurice were prisoners of war in the same stalag. Your Uncle Joseph, who had enlisted at the beginning of the war, was at another stalag near Stettin.

Aida had followed Maurice through all his military deployments since the time he enlisted, and that is how she found herself with him in the south soon after the defeat. He was interned at Camp Gurs, as was she. It was there that she became pregnant with Jackie, who was born at the camp. They then went to Neuvic d'Ussel in the "GTE group of foreign workers" where he worked chopping trees. When they came to deport the GTE workers, Maurice hid. Aida courageously took the train to Pau where her brother lived. I was informed of this in Toulouse. I went to get Maurice where he was hiding in different clothes and carrying false identity papers, and he went to rejoin Aida and her family.

Joseph, like all other prisoners, was allowed to write one letter per month and he had a permission slip to receive one parcel and one response. I took the first permission slip to the *concierge* (superintendent). When Joseph received an answer to his letter with a parcel from his cousin "Thérèse Verdier," he understood well and we continued to correspond until his return.

In October 1942, I returned to the Lycée Victor Hugo and immediately joined the resistance. At that time, apart from the pamphlets calling for the population to revolt and join de Gaulle, I had time on my hands. Your grandfather was very worried about his family in Poland. At the beginning, I went with him several times to the Kommandantur who accepted money to send to Poland. I think they kept the money for themselves, but he still wanted to try.

In the meantime, Rougea had made acquaintance with Léon Groner. He was very kind but came from a very, very simple family. It was during that time that he came to my →

mother to learn "good manners" before Rougea could intro-
duce him to her father. Soon after that they were married.

There were anti-Jewish laws: they kept a census of us, we
had to bring our radios and bicycles to the police station, we
were not allowed to listen to the radio, nor were we allowed to
travel, and we had a curfew. We had to stay in our homes from
8 p.m. to 6 a.m.

On July 15, 1942, I passed my oral exam for my Bachelor's degree and I went home to tell my mother that I was accepted. She immediately told me that we do not speak of these
things because tomorrow there was going to be a roundup.
Mama had sent my brother to hide in the suburb, at the home
of the nurse we had when we were children. Léon Groner also
went into hiding.

The next morning at 5 a.m., the police were knocking at
our door to arrest Mama. My brother Maurice and I were not
on the list because we were French and older than 14 years of
age. Mama had prepared a small parcel and was absolutely quiet.
I wanted us to try to get away, for the police had given her an
hour to prepare herself while they were rounding up our neighbors in this district that was nearly exclusively inhabited by Jews.
We already wore the Jewish star. We could take it off, but
where would we go? And how, without enough money, and for
how long? When she left the house, I ran to Uncle Itche (your
grandfather), rue de Lancry – you know how much I adored
him. The superintendent told me that he was already at the
roundup area (there were provisional ones in each district until
enough Jews were rounded up to fill the bus).

Rougea and her father (your grandfather) were at the fire
station of the rue du Château d'Eau near the mayor's house in
the 10th district.

I asked the police officer, with a smile, for permission to
see my uncle (I showed him my French identity papers). →

I saw them, my uncle and Rougea. She was upset. The superintendent had just come to warn her that Léon Groner had telephoned to say that he had been arrested where he was hiding at La Buissière (in the Loiret section). A woman asked me if I could buy milk for her child. I asked the officer, who agreed. I ran some errands for several people. I then told your grandfather that we could get out, the police were not checking, and here my uncle gave me an answer that I never forgot, nor will I ever forget: "Here they say that they are sending us back from where we came. Thus I will find your aunt and your cousins, who I should never have left behind in Poland." I told him, very agitated, that these are only lies. He answered me, very calmly, "I will take that risk." Rougea didn't want to leave her father and was certain that she would find her husband, who had also been arrested.

You see, Paul, I have often told his story when I speak to students at schools and various institutions, and I always hear these sentences, in Yiddish, in my head.

I was able to hide my mother in the southern zone after her return. Since the months of anti-Jewish laws, I decided to join the Jewish resistance at l'OSE, in the outskirts of Paris and then went with the Jewish Army in Grenoble and Toulouse.

Unfortunately, when we returned, your grandfather, Rougea and Léon Groner did not return, nor did any Bugasjski or Smiétanski who had been deported.

The prisoners returned, as did we.

I went first to the rue des Ecouffes. I came at night and there were no lights in the stairway. I put my key in the lock, but the door was opened. I wanted to turn on the lights but there was no light switch. In the darkness, I realized that everything was emptied. I slept on the floor. The next morning, I was in an empty apartment, bare, even the electrical wires had been ripped out, just like the light switches. Because they were all made of copper. →

When Mama came home, she got busy. We were allowed three wooden beds, a wooden table and three white, wooden chairs. Yes, we were starting a new life. I got busy finding the children that we had hidden and then I left for Palestine in 1947 in Aliyah Daleth (the fourth wave of immigration) with a real passport and a false visa. My brother was in Cyprus where his first son was born.

I returned (to France) in 1953.

Mama, your father's aunt, spent several years in Israel and then she returned. She suffered of Parkinson's for nearly 20 years and died in 1971. My brother died of illness in Israel at the end of 1971.

I am retired but am very busy. I wrote a book on the French resistance which I am sending you; I have just submitted a second edition to print because the first edition has sold out. The second edition compiles 601 biographies. Besides this, I work as a volunteer at the Memorial where I have created an interactive search engine where you can consult the biographies of Jewish French resistance members and see many photos and documents. At this time, you can find the texts only on the internet site **www.memorialdelahoah.org**, but the photos are still available on the internet at the Memorial in Paris.

Dear Paul, I think I have told you what I know for your book. If you still need information and if I can, I will send it to you.

As for the Tomasow family, I cannot give you any more details besides the story of Hélène that I wrote you with the history of Tomasow of Beit Ha'tefousot.

Waiting with courage.

A big hug to you and love to your family,
Frida Wattenberg ✶

The following is an excerpt (translated from French) from the book Vie et mort des juifs sous l'occupation: Récits et témoignages (Life and Death of the Jews under the Occupation: Stories and Witnessed Accounts), *edited by Myriam Foss and Lucien Steinberg and published in 1996. It is from a chapter written by my cousin, Frida Wattenberg, regarding her attempt to save my Grandfather Isaac (her uncle), who was ultimately deported from Paris.*

Not being able to bring over my aunt, my uncle wanted to send her money in Poland. We were so naïve that we went to the Kommandantur, in Opera Square, to deposit money to be sent to my aunt in Poland! I asked my uncle if he believed that this money would be given to her and he answered me that even if there were only a one in a thousand chance, it was worth it to him to try...

After my mother was arrested, I decided to try to find my uncle. I learned that he also had been arrested as well as my cousin (*his daughter*). They parked them in the fire station on Château-d'Eau Street. I tried to visit them by presenting my French papers to the guards, and they let me pass. I then explained to my uncle that he must absolutely run away, for in this neighborhood, it was still possible to do so. He refused. Not for fatalism, but because he was promised that they would send him back from where he came. "They told us that we would be going back to Poland. I should never have left your aunt. At least this way I will find my family..." My uncle had serious cardiac problems and my cousin did not want to abandon him. She refused to run away and, soon afterwards, they were taken away. Soon after that, I heard a hubbub in the Ecouffes Street...I went down to the street and learned, to everyone's amazement, that a man had gotten out from the de Drancy camp. He had been able to get an *Ausweiss* to get →

out because his boss worked for the Germans. My mother also had a boss who made sheep-skinned lined jackets for the Germans. Seeing a possibility, I went to visit this man who, after my explanations, gave me a certificate which might be able to liberate my mother. At first, this certificate allowed us to enter the de Drancy camp and, afterwards, we were told to go home and they refused to return the certificate to us. A few hours later, our mother was returned to us. Later we heard that she had been liberated just in time as she had been selected and had been in line for deportation. Once liberated, my mother believed that she had absolutely nothing else to fear...

In revenge, my cousin was deported and her father soon followed suit. He had been able to throw a letter out the window of the train, which we received, in which he told us that he now knew. He said that he was certain he was going towards his death, that he understood what was really happening, since he had been on this train... ✶

Sicherheitspolizei (SD) Kommando.

   O r l é a n s   Orléans, den 18. Juli 194

IV J - SA 24/42
Ka./Gr.

An den

Befehlshaber der Sicherheits-
polizei und des SD im Bereich des
Militärbefehlshabers in Frankreich
- Abt. IV J -

P a r i s.

                                   2 5. JUL. 1942
                                 22082

Betrifft: Abschub von Juden.

Am 17.7.1942 (Abfahrtzeit 6.15 Uhr) wurden aus dem Lager Pith
809 Juden und 119 Jüdinnen nach dem Osten deportiert. Darunte
fanden sich 193 Juden beiderlei Geschlechts aus dem Bereich de
Kommandeurs Dijon und 52 aus der hiesigen Region.
Die Transportliste, die in zweifacher Ausfertigung dem Trans;
führer Leutnant der Gendarmerie S c h n e i d e r übergeber
wurde, liegt in doppelter Abschrift bei.

                        Der Kommandeur

      Vfg.
                       SS-Hauptsturmführer.
1).
2).
3).
Wv
ZdA

Deportation Documentation (in French and German) for my grandfather, Yankiel (Isaac/Itche)
Wattenberg. He was arrested in Paris on July 16, 1942. He was among a contingent of 1003
Jewish men and women who were then transported by rail to the Auschwitz death camp on
September 16, 1942, where he subsequently perished.

CONVOI N° 33 EN DATE DU 16 SEPTEMBRE 1942 (Yankiel Wa

Ce convoi D 901/28 a quitté la gare du Bourget/Drancy le 16 septembre à 8h55 en direction d'Auschwitz,avec un contingent de 1003 Juifs,sous la direction du chef de transport,le feldwebel Ullmeyer. Tel est le contenu du télex envoyé ce même jour à Eichmann et à Auschwitz par la section anti-juive de la Gestapo (le rédacteur en est le SS Heinrichsohn,le signataire son chef Röthke)/XXVb-164.

Le convoi emportait 586 hommes et 407 femmes. La majorité des hommes et des femmes étant âgés de 40 à 55 ans. La liste,sur papier pelure est en très mauvais état. Du point de vue des nationalités,deux groupes très distincts: d'une part plus de 500 déportés,qui viennent d'être livrés de zone libre par Vichy et transférés de Rivesaltes à Drancy. Ces Juifs sont en grande majorité des Polonais,des Allemands ou des Autrichiens. D'autre part,des Juifs arrêtés dans la région parisienne et,en particulier,au cours des rafles du 14 septembre,qui ont visé les Juifs baltes,bulgares,néerlandais et yougoslaves.

Dans un document daté du 15 septembre (XXVb-163),Jean Leguay,délégué en zone occupée du Secrétaire général à la Police,René Bousquet,écrit au lieutenant SS, Röthke,chef du service anti-juif de la Gestapo: "Le train du 16 septembre sera composé du convoi arrivant de zone libre le 15 septembre,auquel s'ajouteront les Juifs étrangers arrêtés dans la région parisienne au cours des opérations auxquelles vous m'avez demandé de faire procéder". Le convoi,venant de zone libre,dont il est question ici est un train chargé,comme Leguay l'a écrit le 12 septembre à Röthke (XXVI-62),de 600 à 650 Juifs étrangers et qui est arrivé à Drancy le 15 septembre. Nos recherches dans les archives de Rivesaltes nous ont permis de constater qu'un convoi,le 5ème de ce genre,a effectivement quitté Rivesaltes pour Drancy le 14 septembre avec 594 personnes. Ce nombre correspond à celui des personnes déportées de Drancy,le 16 septembre,avec la mention "Rivesaltes" et qui atteint 571 personnes, avec 19 noms barrés en plus.

En ce qui concerne les Juifs arrêtés dans la région parisienne,auxquels Jean Leguay,le plus haut fonctionnaire de police français en zone occupée,fait allusion, un autre document des archives du service anti-juif de la Gestapo établit le processus de la décision de ces arrestations pour ces catégories de Juifs. Il s'agit d'un document du 9 septembre soumis par Röthke à ses supérieurs,Knochen,Lischka et Hagen: " Leguay demanda s'il pouvait arrêter tout de suite à Paris tous les Juifs lithuaniens, esthoniens, lettons, yougoslaves et bulgares. Comme toutes ces catégories entraient en ligne de compte pour la déportation,j'ai répondu affirmativement et demandé leur internement immédiat" (XX Vb-156). La rafle,effectuée par la police parisienne,a donc lieu le 14 septembre et,déjà,le 16 septembre,deux jours plus tard,25 Lettons,88 Lithuaniens,40 Bulgares,14 Yougoslaves et 38 Hollandais partent pour les chambres à gaz d'Auschwitz,où beaucoup périrent dès le 18 septembre. Il est terrible de constater que,dans une Europe en guerre,où l'Allemagne affronte l'URSS,dans un choc qui la mobilise entièrement,il n'a fallu que 8 jours entre la demande de Leguay à Röthke,le 9 septembre,d'arrêter à Paris ces catégories de Juifs et leur assassinat,le 18 septembre,à Auschwitz,à l'autre extrémité de l'Europe. Quelle effroyable efficacité. Ajoutons que Jean Leguay n'a pas été inquiété et qu'il a connu une brillante carrière de dirigeant de firmes internationales, que René Bousquet est devenu Directeur général de la Banque d'Indochine,que Röthke est mort avocat ou conseiller juridique à Wolfsbourg,sans avoir jamais rendu de comptes à la justice,que Lischka,fondé de pouvoir,est à la retraite,que Hagen est directeur commercial et que Knochen est courtier en assurances.

Ce convoi se subdivise en 6 listes:

1/"Drancy 1-escalier1": 32 personnes,Lettons,Lithuaniens,Hollandais. Des familles, les Goedhart d'Amsterdam,Frederik 43,Sarah 35 et leurs 3 enfants,Julius 17,Rose 16 et Robert 6;des enfants sans parents: Micheline 10 et Simone 6 Uboghij,nées à Paris.

2/"Drancy 1-chambre 3": 90 personnes;parmi elles,Joseph 47,Anna 45 Meyer et leurs 4 enfants,Djamba 21,Marcel 15,Djoia 14 et Benjamin 10; Feiga Levine 38 et ses 2 filles Rachel 14 et Ethel 4.

3/"Drancy 1-chambre 4": 80 personnes. Des familles,telle Marguerite Panisel 41 et ses 3 enfants,Robert 9,Elise 8 et Monique 6; telle Maria Tobias 44 et ses 4 enfants,Tekla 19,Albert 13,Hélène 12 et Jacqueline 9.

4/"Partants de dernière heure": 34 personnes.
5/"Drancy 2":Certains noms ne sont suivis d'aucun renseignement d'état-civil. 193
personnes et 81 noms rayés. Des enfants en bas-âge,sans parents,tels les 3 Gradszdajn,
Henri 14,Hélène 10 et Thérèse 7; les 3 Helman,Charlotte 24,Annette 10 et Janric 4;
Estelle Ridel 10 et ses enfants Israel 7 et Huguette 5; Ethel Szajewicz 35 et ses
fillettes Cécile 10 et Aline 2; les 3 enfants Zeligfeld,Henri 14,Hélène 10 et
Simone 2,déportés avec leur grand-mère Paula 57.
6/"camp de Rivesaltes": 571 partants. Aucun lieu de naissance n'est indiqué. Nous
avons pu dénombrer 250 Polonais,201 Allemands,99 Autrichiens,10 Belges,7 Hongrois,
7 apatrides,5 Russes,1 Roumain,1 Lithuanien. De nombreux couples et familles,telle
Pesa Beck 49 et ses 5 enfants Moses 31,Joseph 28,Jenny 22,Leo 21,Isi 19; telle
Bertha Krupnick 31 et ses 2 enfants,Alain 5 et Tcher 4. Dans l'ensemble peu d'enfants en bas âge par rapport aux convois précédents.
   A leur arrivée à Auschwitz,147 femmes furent sélectionnées avec les matricules
19980 à 20126. Environ 300 hommes valides furent sélectionnés pour le travail
avant l'arrivée à Auschwitz. Le reste du convoi fut immédiatement gazé;33 survivants.

MINISTÈRE
DE L'INTÉRIEUR

DIRECTION GÉNÉRALE
DE LA
POLICE NATIONALE

P.N. Cab. A N°540

ÉTAT FRANÇAIS

PARIS, le 12 Septembre 1942

X XV-62

LE SOUS-PREFET
Délégué dans les Territoires Occupés
du SECRETAIRE GENERAL à la POLICE

à Monsieur l'Obersturmführer ROTKE
31 bis, Avenue Foch

P A R I S

   Je vous confirme ma communication téléphonique de
ce jour :

   Un convoi venant de zone libre et composé d'environ 600 à 650 Juifs étrangers, passera la ligne de démar-
cation :

     à VIERZON le 15 Septembre 1942 à 1 h 51
     Départ de VIERZON le 15 Septembre à 2 h 40
     Arrivée au BOURGET-DRANCY le 15/9/42 à 10 h 23

   Je vous prie de vouloir bien prendre les disposi-
tions nécessaires pour que la Feldgendarmerie soit avisée
de ce convoi.

Vis.

NDLR Communication du délégué en zone occupée du Secrétaire-général à la Police
du gouvernement de Vichy,Jean Leguay,au chef du service anti-juif de la Gestapo.

NOM : .... W A T E N B E R G ....

PRÉNOMS : .... Jankiel, Dawid ....

Date et lieu | ...... 1885 à Brzeriny (Pol) ......
de naissance |

.... N° du **Dossier juif** : 16/010

SEXE : .... masculin ....

NATIONALITÉ : ...... Polonaise ......

PROFESSION : ...... sans ......

ADRESSE : .... 36, rue de Lancry ....

.... 10° ....

SITUATION de famille : ...... marié ......

CONJOINT : .... juif ....

	Prénoms	Date et lieu de naissance	Nationalité
ENFANTS de moins de 15 ans et à charge			

INFIRMITÉS : ....

SERVICES de GUERRE : ...... Arrêté le 16.7.42
Convoi du 16.9.42

SITUATION | ....
administrative | ....
de l'étranger | ....

N° du casier central : .... I.597.296 ....

REMARQUES PARTICULIÈRES : ....

....

....

265-E — Imp. Chaix (B). — 1591-41

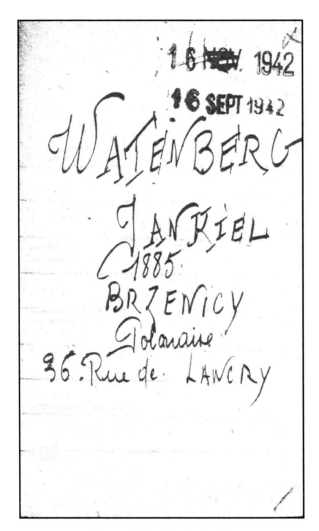

My grandfather's final train ticket.

Selig WASSERSTROM · Ita WASSERSZTAJN
Martin WASSERZUG 1896 · Bella WASS
Monique WASSREICH 1937 · Raymon
Jankiel WATENBERG 1885 · Fritz WAT
Maurice WAYMAN 1910 · Isaak WAYNI
Jakob WAYS 1903 · Edith WAYSBROT 1935
Israël WAYSSLER 1879 · Beila WAYZNER 1

Grandfather's name on Wall of Memories at Holocaust Museum in Paris.

Leon Groner
époux de
Ida Wattenbp
(Rougea)

CONVOI N° 6 EN DATE DU 17 JUILLET 1942

Ce convoi a quitté le camp de Pithiviers,avec un contingent de 809 hommes et de 119 femmes,soit 928 personnes déportées. Un télex du kommando de la Sipo-SD (la police nazie) d'Orléans le confirme le 18 juillet à la section anti-juive (IVJ) de la Gestapo à Paris. Il précise aussi que,parmi les déportés, 193 Juifs et Juives avaient été envoyées par le kommando de la Sipo-SD de Dijon et que 52 autres provenaient du kommando d'Orléans lui-même. Le télex ajoute que deux listes originales ont été remises au chef du convoi,le lieutenant de gendarmerie Schneider.

La liste des noms est dans un état presqu'illisible. Il s'agit de papier pelure et les noms sont à peu près indéchiffrables; le carbone était de couleur violette. Sont précisés le nom,le prénom,la date et le lieu de naissance,la profession et la ville du domicile. L'orthographe des noms est extrêmement fantaisiste.

La plupart des déportés proviennent de la région parisienne.

La nationalité n'est pas précisée. Mais en parcourant les lieux de naissance des déportés,on constate que,dans leur très grande majorité,il s'agit de localités polonaises.

La tranche d'âge la plus fournie se situe entre 33 et 42 ans (550 sur 928 déportés). Des adolescents entre 16 et 22 ans accompagnent leurs parents; on en compte 141. Il y a même quelques enfants plus jeunes encore,telle Marie-Louise Warenbron,née à Paris,le 27 avril 1930 et qui n'a que 12 ans,ou Rebecca Nowodworski,née à Luxembourg ,le 13 septembre 1928 et qui n'a pas 14 ans.

Deux documents de la Gestapo concernent ce convoi: le XXVb-65 du 14 juillet et le télex réglementaire (XXVb-75) du 17 juillet,adressé de Paris par la section anti-juive de la Gestapo à Eichmann à Berlin,à l'Inspection des camps à Oranienburg et au commandant d'Auschwitz. Dans ce télex,il est indiqué que le convoi a quitté Pithiviers,le 17 juillet,à 6h.15 avec 928 Juifs,dont 119 femmes.

A leur arrivée à Auschwitz,le 19 juillet,les 809 hommes ont reçu les matricules 48880 à 49688 et les 119 femmes les matricules 9550 à 9668.

Il y aurait eu,en 1945,18 survivants de ce convoi.

Betrifft: Abschub von Juden.

Am 17.7.1942 (Abfahrtzeit 6.15 Uhr) wurden aus dem Lager Pithiviers 809 Juden und 119 Jüdinnen nach dem Osten deportiert. Darunter befanden sich 193 Juden beiderlei Geschlechts aus dem Bereich des Kommandeurs Dijon und 52 aus der hiesigen Region.

Die Transportliste, die in zweifacher Ausfertigung dem Transportführer Leutnant der Gendarmerie S c h n e i d e r übergeben wurde, liegt in doppelter Abschrift bei.

Der Kommandeur

Vfg.

1)

SS-Hauptsturmführer.

La note du 18 juillet de la Sipo-SD d'Orléans prévenant
la section anti-juive à Paris que 809 Juifs et 119
Juives ont été déportées à L'Est,le 17 juillet

Deportation Document for Yankiel's daughter, Rougea, and her husband, Leon Groner.

Two poems written my uncle, Maurice Wattenberg, which bespoke the sadness of his heart as he reflected on the destruction of our entire family in the Holocaust.

La plus grande tragédie de l'histoire de l'humanité

Dans un océan de sang
De mon peuple et les autres
Depuis hélas trop longtemps
Malgré les prophètes et les apôtres.

Sans essence humaine
Les animaux parlants ont sévi
Guidés par la rage et la haine
Et des millions de gens ont péri

Ni au ciel ni sous terre
Et pendant le silence du monde
Parents, soeurs et frères
Anéantis par la bête immonde.

D'un peuple sans défense ni armes
Les assassins savourent la gloire
Maise malgré les souffrances et les larmes
Les rescapés gardent l'espoir
En un monde de paix
Où la loi du plus fort
Ne règnera plus sur l'humanité
Et plus jamais de marche de troupes de la mort.

The Biggest Tragedy in the History of Humanity

In an ocean of blood
Of my people and others
Since alas too long a time
In spite of the prophets and the apostles

Without human essence
The speaking animals prevailed
Guided by rage and hatred
And millions of people perished

Neither in heaven nor under earth
And during the silence of the world
Parents, sisters and brothers
Destroyed by the foul beast.

From a people without defense or weapons
The assassins savored the glory
But despite the suffering and the tears
The escaped keep hope
Of a world of peace
Where the law of the strongest
Will no longer reign over humanity
And never again will the death troops march.

Cinquante ans
Cinquante ans que je dors peu or pas
J'écoute le silence de la nuit
Il me semble que c'est là
Une foule qui marche sans bruit.

La marche de six millions d'âmes
Six millions de martyrs
Et qui passés par les flammes
N'ont même pas de sépultures.

Alors, tel l'arc-en-ciel on pouvait voir
Accrochées aux nuages trèês haut
A l'horizon malgré la nuit noire
Des lettres enflammées formant un seul mot
Pourquoi ??!

Aucune réponse à ce jour
Je n'entends aucune voix
Contre la destruction de mes amours
Pouvant calmer mon désarroi.

Fifty Years
Fifty years I'm sleeping little or not at all
I'm listening to the silence of the night
It seems that it was there
That a crowd of people walked without sound.

The walk of six million souls
Six million martyrs
And who pass through the flames
Don't even have a grave.

Then, what a rainbow we could see
Attached to the clouds way up high
In the horizon despite the black night
Inflamed letters forming a single word
Why ??!

Not an answer to this day
I do not hear a single voice
Against the destruction of my loved ones
Able to calm my turmoil. ✶

This is a letter that I wrote with the help of Morty Howard, a friend of mine, to the New York Times in 2007. It is an expression of my hostility at the audacity of the President of Iran who came to visit the United States and continually stated that the Holocaust did not occur.

Dear Editor,

I am shocked and chagrined that you would devote time and space to the President of Iran when he visited New York.

When he was asked, "How and why can you say that the Holocaust did not happen?" you did not take him to task!

Your editorials are always slanted towards criticizing our administration and you always have suggestions as to what we should do or what we should have done. I am a Holocaust survivor! I could list so many things that happened to my family. How they were slaughtered one after the other either by gas or by pistol. I could spend hours describing how my mother and I lived in order to survive. However, it might fall on deaf ears. Why, I ask, would you not challenge this sick and biased power-hungry "nut" to travel with a group of reputable people to the former concentration camps to see what took place? Those ovens and barracks were not put there recently as movie props.

Why would you not face him directly and challenge him to prove this tragedy did not happen? Why do you run and hide and/or suggest we meet and listen to his tirades without asking the important questions, ie, "Why do you, the President of Iran, believe the Holocaust did not happen – that it is all a lie – and why do you want to blow Israel off the face of the Earth and kill every Jew throughout the world?!! Why? Explain to everyone why this would be a good thing and how it would benefit the world."

Mr. Editor, instead of trying to find fault with those who are governing the greatest country in the world, you should stop making condescending overtures to those who are doing everything possible to defeat our nation. You should try to become a team player. Shame on you! ✴

Unfortunately, in the years since I wrote the above letter to *The New York Times*, denial of the Holocaust has continued to grow. There are those who would deny that six million Jews were brutally tortured and murdered in the most depraved and despicable ways while the German people looked the other way. This is no doubt why General Eisenhower, upon finding the victims of the death camps, ordered that all possible photographs be taken, and that the German people from surrounding villages be ushered through the camps and even made to bury the dead. He knew that down the road of history, someone would get up and say this never happened. But the Jewish culture, with its brilliant intellectual life, creativity and talent, and its remarkable contributions to the world in all areas of life – science, art, international trade, not to mention 129 Nobel Laureates even though we represent only about .02% of the world's population – continues to flourish. This, in spite of those who would deny the Holocaust and destroy us still. So now, more than ever, with Iran, among others, claiming the Holocaust to be a myth, it is imperative that the world never forgets.

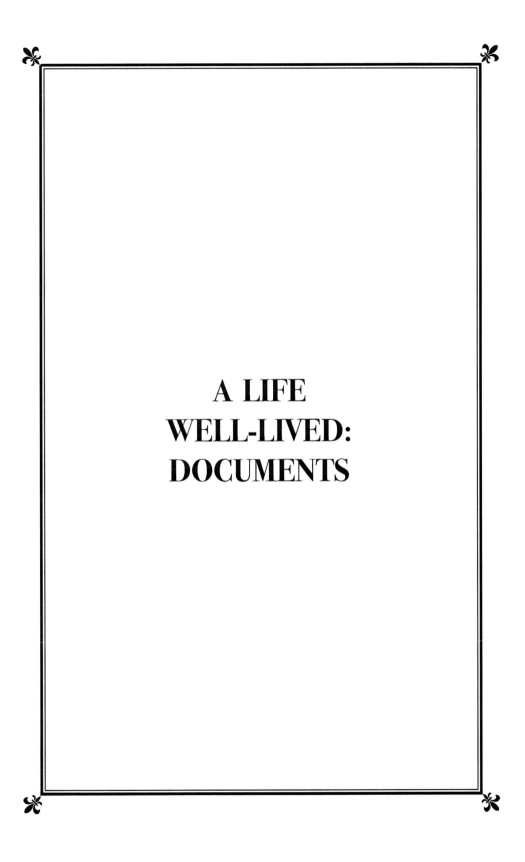

A LIFE
WELL-LIVED:
DOCUMENTS

A family's flight to success

By FRANK MAZZA

IT'S NOT YOUR typical rags-to-riches story, but it begins in a small men's wear shop in Paris and ends in a swank New York showroom of a multi-million-dollar fashion house.

Brothers Paul and Gary Wattenberg are the heirs and operating officers of Leon of Paris—a $20 million international design, manufacture and licensing fashion enterprise of men's and women's wear employing more than 600 worldwide. But to Paul, 47, of Great Neck, L.I., and Gary, 36, a year-round resident of Westhampton Beach, L.I., Leon of Paris wasn't always that way.

As the elder, Paul remembers his homeland in France when Leon of Paris was only a dream in the eyes of his dad in the late 1930s. He remembers as a child how the Nazis shattered that dream, the flight, the struggle in a new world and the eventual attainment of financial success and professional recognition.

"We lived in the back of the shop in Paris," Paul recounted, while sipping coffee in his office on the 14th floor of 1280 Sixth Ave. at 51st St. "There was my dad, (Leon), one cutter, one shipper, one assistant and 12 operators." The operators didn't work in the small shop, but did their sewing in their homes.

Known, then as the House of Leon, the firm began to prosper and just before the outbreak of World War II, moved to a new location in Paris large enough to house all, including 25 operators, under one roof. "It was a sort of mini plant," Paul smiled.

In 1938 the elder Wattenberg visited the U.S. as a potential site for expansion. But, before he could return, war had engulfed Europe and he was trapped on American soil. By June, Paris was surrounded by the Germans. Paul and his mom tried to escape to neutral Portugal through southern France and Spain, but were captured by the Germans only a few miles from Paris and returned.

"We had heard stories of what the Nazis were doing to Jews back in Germany, but of course didn't believe them," Paul said. "Who could believe such stories at that time?" he shrugged. Only nine years old at the time, Paul grimaces when he recalls the scene of his mother sewing the Star of David onto the sleeve of his clothing. All Jews in Paris were made to wear the religious sign by order of the occupying Nazis.

Left profound mark

The scene left such a profound mark that Paul, together with his wife, Linda, vowed to become active in Jewish charities, particularly those aiding children. Both are tireless workers—raising funds for Hadassah, the organization which finances hospitals in Israel; and the Deborah League, which supports a New Jersey children's hospital.

Paul and Mrs. Wattenberg also are volunteer fund raisers for the Federation of Jewish Philanthropies and a daughter, Debbie, a pre-med student, carries on the tradition as a volunteer worker at North Shore Hospital, Manhasset, L.I.

"When my husband tells us of the suffering his family—and thousands like them—was subjected to during the war, we realize how fortunate we are to be Americans," said Mrs. Wattenberg.

"We also remind our children of their obligations to people less fortunate than we are. They, thankfully, agree with our philosophy." The Wattenbergs have two other children, son Lee, 17, and daughter Wendy, 13.

But, back in March 1941, the stories of concentration camps and extermination centers became more and more persistent. Young Paul and his mom decided to attempt another escape. This time, with the help of the French Underground, they made it to Marseilles.

By late summer, Mom and Paul made it across the Iberian Peninsula to Lisbon and aboard one of the last refuge boats that sailed for America. Three months later the U.S. entered the war and Atlantic crossings of refuge ships ceased. The young Hyman Korn is today, the sage Justice of the New York State Supreme Court.

The re-united Wattenbergs settled in the Bronx; Leon, opened a small shop at 1 Union Square and called it, naturally, Leon of Paris. In 1942 Gary was born to the Wattenbergs. The post war period was a boom to the clothing business with men trading in their khakis for blue serge and gabardine.

While Paul and Gary were schooled through DeWitt Clinton High School and NYU, Leon of Paris progressed and gradually moved uptown along Fifth Ave. First to 17th St., then 18th and each time to bigger and better quarters.

In 1960 the elder Wattenberg died. Paul, who had been working in the shop part-time, took over as president. Paul expanded the market for Leon of Paris and after a few years moved the business to his present plush location.

Under the leadership of Paul and Gary, Leon of Paris broadened its market to deal in both men's and women's attire and expanded its list of fashions able to include sweaters, ties, shoes, tennis attire, shirts, sportswear and perfume.

Designer persuaded

Adolfo, designer of women's wear, was persuaded by the Wattenberg brothers to expand his field of expertise and join the modern, functional Leon of Paris fashion house. Under the merger, the cost of Adolfo styles was significantly reduced.

Gary was asked if giving up the Leon of Paris label was a hard decision to make. "Yes," he answered, "I was filled with mixed emotions." He said it was difficult to end a tradition begun by his dad, but was sure his father would have agreed.

Paul Wattenberg explains the ins and outs of the fashion business from his Leon of Paris office in Manhattan.

Linda Wattenberg shows off plaque her husband received.

The Daily News, Sunday, February 18, 1979

"A Family's Flight to Success" article from The Daily News,
Sunday, February 18, 1979 by Frank Mazza

It's not your typical rages-to-riches story, but it began in a small men's wear shop in Paris and ends in a swank New York showroom of a multi-million-dollar fashion house.

Brothers Paul and Gary Wattenberg are the heirs and operating officers of Leon of Paris – a $30 million international design, manufacture and licensing fashion enterprise of men's and women's wear employing more than 600 worldwide. But to Paul, 47, of Great Neck, L.I. and Gary, 36, a year-round resident of Westhampton Beach, L.I., Leon of Paris wasn't always that way.

As the elder, Paul remembers his homeland in France when Leon of Paris was only a dream in the eyes of his dad in the late 1930's. He remembers as a child how the Nazis shattered that dream, the flight, the struggle in a new world and the eventual attainment of financial success and professional recognition.

"We lived in the back of the shop in Paris," Paul recounted, while sipping coffee in his office on the 14th floor of 1290 Sixth Ave. at 51st St. "There was my dad, (Leon), one cutter, one shipper, one assistant and 12 operators. The operators didn't work in the small shop, but did their sewing in their homes."

Known then as the House of Leon, the firm began to prosper and just before the outbreak of World War II, moved to a new location in Paris large enough to house all, including 25 operators, under one roof. "It was a sort of mini plant," Paul smiled.

In 1939 the elder Wattenberg visited the U.S. as a potential site for expansion. But, before he could return, war had engulfed Europe and he was trapped on American soil. By June, Paris was surrounded by the Germans. Paul and his mom tried to escape to neutral Portugal through southern France and Spain, but were captured by the Germans only a few miles from Paris and returned. →

"We had heard stories of what the Nazis were doing to Jews back in Germany, but of course didn't believe them," Paul said. "Who could believe such stories at that time?" he shrugged.

Only nine years old at the time, Paul grimaces when he recalls the scene of his mother sewing the Star of David onto the sleeve of his clothing. All Jews in Paris were made to wear the religious sign by order of the occupying Nazis.

Left profound mark

The scene left such a profound mark that Paul, together with his wife, Linda, vowed to become active in Jewish charities, particularly those aiding children. Both are tireless workers raising funds for Hadassah, the organization which finances hospitals in Israel; and the Deborah League, which supports a New Jersey children's hospital.

Paul and Mrs. Wattenberg also are volunteer fund raisers for the Federation of Jewish Philanthropies and a daughter, Debbie, a pre-med student, carries on the tradition as a volunteer worker at North Shore Hospital, Manhasset, L.I.

"When my husband tells us of the suffering his family – and thousands like them – was subjected to during the war, we realize how fortunate we are to be Americans," said Mrs. Wattenberg.

"We also remind our children of their obligations to people less fortunate than we are. They, thankfully, agree with our philosophy." The Wattenbergs have two other children, son Lee, 17, and daughter Wendy, 13.

But, back in March 1941, the stories of concentration camps and extermination centers became more and more persistent. Young Paul and his mom decided to attempt another escape. This time, with the help of the French Underground, they made it to Marseilles. →

By late summer, Mom and Paul made it across the Iberian Peninsula to Lisbon and aboard one of the last refuge boats that sailed for America. Three months later the U.S. entered the war and Atlantic crossings of refuge ships ceased. The young Hyman Korn is today the sage Justice of the New York State Supreme Court.

The re-united Wattenbergs settled in the Bronx. Leon opened a small shop at 1 Union Square and called it, naturally, Leon of Paris. In 1942 Gary was born to the Wattenbergs. The post war period was a boom to the clothing business with men trading in their khakis for blue serge and gabardine.

While Paul and Gary were schooled through DeWitt Clinton High School and NYU, Leon of Paris progressed and gradually moved uptown along Fifth Ave., first to 17th St., then 18th and each time to bigger and better quarters.

In 1960, the elder Wattenberg died. Paul, who had been working in the shop part-time, took over as president. Paul expanded the market for Leon of Paris and after a few years moved the business to his present plush location.

Under the leadership and Paul and Gary, Leon of Paris broadened its market to deal in both men's and women's attire and expanded its list of fashionables to include sweaters, ties, shoes, tennis attire, shirts, sportswear and perfume.

Designer persuaded

Adolfo, designer of women's wear, was persuaded by the Wattenberg brothers to expand his field of expertise and join the modern, functional Leon of Paris fashion house. Under the merger, the cost of Adolfo styles was significantly reduced.

Gary was asked if giving up the Leon of Paris label was a hard decision to make. "Yes," he answered. "I was filled with mixed emotions." He said it was difficult to end a tradition begun by his dad, but was sure his father would have agreed. ✴

Article in newsletter by The Associated Men's Wear Retailers of New York *on the occasion of my being presented with the Man of the Year Award, April 24, 1979.*

Paul Wattenberg, President of Adolfo and Leon of Paris, has been designated 1979 Man of the Year by the Associated Men's Wear Retailers of New York and will receive the Award on Tuesday, April 24, 1979, at the Harmonie Club, New York City.

This is the 32nd year that the Awards Committee of our Association has chosen a Man of the Year. By definition he is the man who, in the judgment of the Committee, has done most to help further the progress of the industry and bring credit to men's wear through his efforts in the community and the nation. The roster includes men from all segments of the trade. In singling these men out for recognition, the Association has encouraged improved trade citizenship and industry leadership. The Committee is proud to add the name of Paul Wattenberg to its list of illustrious trade citizens.

Paul Wattenberg has enhanced the success of the men's wear industry and his own company through his first-hand knowledge of every facet of manufacturing men's clothing. His career in men's wear started when, as a teen-ager, he learned much of what he knows from his father, Leon, who founded the House of Leon in Paris, France in 1930. The elder Wattenberg established the House's American operation, Leon of Paris, in New York City in 1939. Since becoming President of Leon of Paris in 1959, Paul has contributed to the expansion of the firm's activities through his innovative talents in design, sales, finance, administration and marketing. In 1960, he formed the John Hampton division of the company and in 1975 he introduced Adolfo Men's Wear, designed by Adolfo, the internationally famous couturier. As President of Adolfo, Paul has added new looks and concepts to the clothing industry, that →

have had a striking impact on retail sales. Guided by the business philosophy that every retailer and manufacturer must have a "raison d'être" in order to fill a specific need in a specific market, he has employed his exceptional creative talents to bring increased prosperity, greater fashion leadership and influence to his company, all of which has been to the benefit of the entire industry.

Mr. Wattenberg's commitment to New York City and its men's wear industry has earned him a letter of commendation from Governor Carey and a proclamation from the Borough of Manhattan. Involved in industry, community and philanthropic organizations, he is a member of the Board of Directors of both the Clothing Manufacturers Association of America and the New York Clothing Manufacturers Association, a member of the national panel of the American Arbitration Association and an active participant in the work of the United Jewish Appeal, the Federation of Jewish Philanthropies, the United Fund and the Alexander Goode-Ben Goldman Lodge of B'nai B'rith.

Paul graduated from New York University in 1953 with a degree in Business Administration. He and his wife Linda live in Lake Success, New York with son Lee and daughters Debbie and Wendy. His brother Gary, as Executive Vice President of Adolfo, shares in all of the important responsibilities that have contributed to the growth and success of the company and joins with Paul in many of his industry and philanthropic activities. ✱

Isidore S. Immerman
Counsel-Director

Man of the Year Speech

Ladies and Gentlemen - Members of the Association and Dear Friends,

I would like to thank the Association of the New York Retailers for this great honor bestowed upon me.

I must say that I was elated and flattered when the committee called to advise me that I had been chosen as their "Man of the Year" for 1979.

This award is indeed a most cherished honor. An honor, though, which in my heart, will always be shared with my brother Gary, whose untiring efforts have been a major factor in the growth and success of our company (Gary, take a bow – rise).

During the last four years, we have all been witness to significant changes within the men's wear industry. As the '70s are rapidly coming to a close, I see the 1980s as the decade of what I call raison d'être. Raison d'être means a reason for being, a reason for existing within our industry.

A new challenge for all of us

The raison d'être for all of us in the '80s will be specialization. No longer will we be able to "straddle the fence" insofar as fashion direction is concerned. The consumer of the '80s is going to be more sophisticated and demanding, therefore, making it incumbent upon every retailer and manufacturer to take a position with regard to the fashion direction he sees for his company or his stores.

No longer will the jack-of-all-trades be able to function as in the past. The old saying, "You can't be all things to all people" will be more meaningful than ever before. Every merchant will have to select a more specific marketing direction and cater to a special customer within his marketplace.

For merchants with talent and expertise, there will be opportunity for growth and success. Pinpoint your market and be the best at catering to that lifestyle. It's impossible to be all things to all people.

Let's look at another challenge facing our industry in the '80s.

The influx of imports is damaging to everyone in the apparel business. International trade is a fact of life. World trade is necessary.

But it is unnecessary for the uncontrolled influx of imported apparel from low labor countries that could eventually put two million needle and textile workers on welfare. The burden would be intolerable.

We have to realize that every time someone loses a job in any American industry, the retail community is also losing a potential consumer.

All of us in the related textile and apparel business should use our combined efforts to limit imports by quota agreements. Washington has to hear from all of us, for, as a group, we will be heard. In fact we are already being heard and the results are leading to new quota agreements. These better quotas will enable our domestic apparel industry to cope, survive, and even flourish.

A closely related problem is over-reaction to foreign fashion direction. Why are retailers and manufacturers continually intimidated by European designers and concepts? Should we let dictates emanating from 3000 miles away determine what is right or wrong for the American male?

We need not follow. We can lead and be fashion innovators – interpreting and creating right here in New York specific fashion statements for the American male – made and created in the U.S.A.

In launching Adolfo menswear, we have proven that American creativity is valid.

Before I proceed further, I would like, at this time, to mention the New York retailer who is the most dedicated and talented and an extremely knowledgeable merchant. One who has had to overcome difficult problems, more numerous and more serious than anywhere else in the country. In spite of many hardships, he has survived, thrived, succeeded and can look optimistically to the future.

Please let us extend a tribute to the Association of New York Retailers.

Standing before you, I recall the late 1930s when I was a young boy scampering about my father's small warehouse in Paris. Who could have dreamt then that, here tonight in 1979, I would be honored by my peers.

How sad that my father did not live to see his company's success!!!!

But le destin d'homme, or man's destiny, is not ours to plot.

An evening like tonight proves to me that America is the great land of opportunity. Any young man who can conceive an idea, believe in it, will be able – with tenacity – to achieve his goal.

But behind every success story there are usually others standing in the wings who are greatly responsible for helping a man reach his goal.

In my case, they are my beautiful and talented wife, Linda (take a bow), my handsome son, Lee, and my beautiful and lovable daughters, Debbie and Wendy (Guys, please stand up).

And I cannot for a moment forget to thank one person here tonight – were it not for her vision and faith, this event would not have been possible at all – she is my constant mentor and has continually been a very courageous human being throughout her life – my mother.

Thank you, Mom.

The term "Man of the Year" does indeed mean different things to different people. To me, it is an honor which I will forever cherish.

I would like to thank everyone for participating tonight and making this one of the most beautiful and memorable evenings of my life.

THANK YOU. ✱

*My wife ANN and I congratulate the Associated Men's
Wear Retailers of New York for selecting*

PAUL WATTENBERG

PRESIDENT OF LEON OF PARIS

AS MAN OF THE YEAR FOR 1979

*I can think of no other individual in our industry whose
SOUL, HEART and MIND are dedicated day and night
to the creation of beautifully styled ADOLFO fashion
clothing for the American consumer.*

*PAUL'S endless drive for perfection in everything he
does is an expression of his great GENIUS. He is an
HONOR to our INDUSTRY, to NEW YORK CITY and to
AMERICA and I am proud to be associated with him.*

HAROLD PLATT
Secretary/Treasurer
LEON OF PARIS CO., INC.

Associated Men's Wear Retailers

PAUL WATTENBERG
"Fashion knows no season:
if fashion is right, it will sell—
regardless of the time of year."
This adaptability, the instinctive ability to know
when a certain fashion "look" has had it,
has enabled Wattenberg, shown below in the cutting room
of his Leon of Paris factory, to keep his
finger on the pulse of American male fashion wants.
"Men no longer feel they have to look the same,"
and it's to this new search for an individualized
"boutique" look that Wattenberg caters—
as he has for the past twenty years.
His own suit—shaped, close to the body
(près de corps, he calls it)—illustrates the look
he favors: Thirties lapels, angled flap pockets,
wide-flared-bottom trousers,
and a slim, shaped, tubular effect.

Gentlemen's Quarterly, 1976.

Gentleman's Quarterly Magazine: *Tomorrow Designers Today*, 1976.

PAUL WATTENBERG

"Fashion knows no season: if fashion is right, it will sell – regardless of the time of year."

This adaptibility, the instinctive ability to know when a certain fashion "look" has had it, has enabled Wattenberg, shown below in the cutting room of his Leon of Paris factory, to keep his finger on the pulse of American male fashion wants.

"Men no longer feel they have to look the same," and it's to this new search for an individualized "boutique" look that Wattenberg caters – as he has for the past twenty years. His own suit – shaped, close to the body (*prés de corps* as he calls it) – illustrates the look he favors: Thirties lapels, angled flap pockets, wide-flared bottom trousers, and a slim, shaped tubular effect. ✱

VIEWPOINT

PAUL WATTENBERG
PRESIDENT
ADOLFO

Leon of Paris, together with its Adolfo affiliate, has grown substantially in recent years with a mix of clothing, outerwear, shirts, slacks, sweaters and sportswear in a European-inspired designer look.

Wattenberg has developed a very specific VIEWPOINT about selling and merchandising, particularly designer looks, in the men's wear business.

He believes that retailers are getting what they pay for in retail sales staff and that well-paid staffs are outperforming poorly-paid ones in both department and specialty operations. He thinks further that department stores, particularly, are moving to upgrade sales personnel.

His judgment is that specialty and department stores which operate on specialty store concepts pay best and that their results in the clothing area justify it to the point where other stores, now selling half of their clothing off price are moving to upgrade sales staff.

MW: Has the controversy over classification versus shop selling of designer names at retail shaken out at this point?
WATTENBERG: Well, it's really determined by the type of retail store. I personally prefer the shop concept; department stores have the real estate to do it, most specialty stores don't. So the specialist has to compensate with the personal service, rapport ethic he has with his customers and walk him through the various departments in which he's located the various looks.

MW: Are there too many designer names?
WATTENBERG: What's too many? It still boils down to the same thing: how professional is the resource. If he's slapping a name tag on the sleeve then that name will come and it'll go——It's happening already. As in everything else, the idea begins with a credible product, showing individuality and proper cut, make and trim. A designer name will make a good product super but the product must be there.

MW: Do retailers really know how to sell designer?
WATTENBERG: That is the central problem in retailing today because it relates to the quality of personnel at retail. There are

two types of department stores, for example. The first, like Saks Fifth Avenue, model themselves on the specialty store concept, know the product, give service and get paid for it. Good clothing salesmen make $30-40,000 in these stores compared with the salesmen in the class 2 department stores who make $15-20,000 and the sales show it. Though I will say that department stores are beginning to realize that and are upgrading the quality of sales help as they see a branch with a good manager begin to outperform the rest of the group. There is a thrust to upgrade people.

There is a similar distinction in specialty stores. The single store operation involves the owner on the selling floor. He can project what he's bought to the customer he knows and convince him of its rightness. In a multiple-store specialty operation, the owner can't be on the floor but he remembers those days and gets people to carry it through.

Here are some numbers which support the thesis: about 50 percent of clothing in department stores is sold off-price, a much higher percentage than in specialty stores; buyers in specialty stores tend to have 15-20 years experience compared with a department store buyer who just moved from dishes. The result is that the buyer with taste level and experience will take "chances" which really aren't dangerous because he knows what he is doing while the inexperienced guy has to play it safe so the presentation lacks snap.

MW: Which designer classification will do best this fall?
WATTENBERG: Sport coats, no question they have been the greatest growth areas

in the past two fall seasons. I think that jackets will be 35-40 percent of open-to-buys this fall after slumping from 35 percent down to 5 percent in recent years.

Surprisingly, it hasn't come at the expense of clothing. There are more dollars being spent. The key is that clothing has held steady over the past few years while the population has increased. Also, the play of second incomes is important here. I believe that when the figures are in, overall apparel expenditures will show tremendous growth.

Look at the growth in sportswear and active looks. Where's the money coming from? Young people can't afford housing, car sales are slumping and historically, that's been a good time for apparel.

MW: You've added several price points and styles of designer lines. Do you want to be the General Motors of the designer business?
WATTENBERG: No, we have three divisions for different looks and customers. They also provide synergism because they are structured as three separate "companies" and the individual focus allows us to know about changes in one direction or another. We can put resources in natural shoulder if that's coming on strongly, or in young men's if that's happening.

MW: Are you deepening your involvement in sportswear as a hedge?
WATTENBERG: We plan to get into more sportswear. We learned a lot from our first year in the business. I think we jumped in too early because of demand. We're going to do it right in terms of product and delivery this year.

MW: Do stores till want coordinated packages or are they more comfortable with buying on their own?
WATTENBERG: I like the concept personally. The refinement of the concept is really Utopia. Now, the avant-garde guy who represents 1 or 2 percent of the business can put the looks together for a very specific customer type but most people have the resource put the package together for them.

By refinement of the concept, I mean avoiding the situation where you put together slacks, tops, sweaters and jackets and vests and everything sells but the vests. What does the retailer, or the manufacturer for that matter, do with the vests? They don't go with anything now because you've sold the rest. ■

Interview in *Men's Wear*, 1987

Viewpoint Interview in Men's Wear, *1987*
"Paul Wattenberg: President (of) Adolfo"

Leon of Paris, together with its Adolfo affiliate, has grown substantially in recent years with a mix of clothing, outwear, shirts,
slacks, sweaters and sportswear in a European-inspired designer look.

Wattenberg has developed a very specific VIEWPOINT
about selling and merchandising, particularly designer looks, in
the men's wear business.

He believes that retailers are getting what they pay for in retail sales staff and that well-paid staffs are outperforming poorly-
paid ones in both department and specialty operations. He thinks
further that department stores, particularly, are moving to upgrade sales personnel.

His judgment is that specialty and department stores which operate on specialty store concepts pay best and that their results in
the clothing area justify it to the point where other stores, now selling half of their clothing off price are moving to upgrade sales staff.

MW: Has the controversy over classification versus shop selling
of designer names at retail shaken out at this point?
WATTENBERG: Well, it's really determined by the type of retail store. I personally prefer the shop concept: department stores
have the real estate to do it, most specialty stores don't. So the
specialist has to compensate with the personal service, rapport
ethic he has with his customers and walk him through the various departments in which he's located the various looks.
MW: Are there too many designer names?
WATTENBERG: What's too many? It still boils down to the
same thing: how professional is the resource. If he's slapping a
name tag on the sleeve then that name will come and it'll go—
it's happening already. As in everything else, the idea begins with
a credible product, showing individuality and proper cut, →

make and trim. A designer name will make a good product super but the product must be there.

MW: Do retailers really know how to sell designer?

WATTENBERG: That is the central problem in retailing today because it relates to the quality of personnel at retail. There are two types of department stores, for example. The first, like Saks Fifth Avenue, model themselves on the specialty store concept, know the product, give service and get paid for it. Good clothing salesmen make $30 – 40,000 in these stores compared with the salesmen in the class 2 department stores who make $15 – 20,000 and the sales show it. Though I will say that department stores are beginning to realize that and are upgrading the quality of sales help as they see a branch with a good manager begin to outperform the rest of the group. There is a thrust to upgrade people.

There is a similar distinction in specialty stores. The single store operation involves the owner on the selling floor. He can project what he's bought to the customer he knows and convince him of its rightness. In a multiple-store specialty operation, the owner can't be on the floor but he remembers those days and gets people to carry it through.

Here are some numbers which support the thesis: about 50 percept of clothing in department stores is sold off-price, a much higher percentage than in specialty stores; buyers in specialty stores tend to have 15-20 years experience compared with a department store buyer who just moved from dishes. The result is that the buyer with taste level and experience will take "chances" which really aren't dangerous because he knows what he is doing while the inexperienced guy has to play it safe, so the presentation lacks snap.

MW: Which designer classification will do best this fall?

WATTENBERG: Sport coats, no question they have been the greatest growth areas in the past two fall seasons. I think that jackets will be 35-40 percent of open-to-buys this fall after slumping from 35 percent down to 5 percent in recent years. →

Surprisingly, it hasn't come at the expense of clothing. There are more dollars being spent. The key is that clothing has held steady over the past few years while the population has increased. Also, the play of second incomes is important here. I believe that when the figures are in, overall apparel expenditures will show tremendous growth.

Look at the growth in sportswear and active looks. Where's the money coming from? Young people can't afford housing, car sales are slumping and historically, that's been a good time for apparel.

MW: You've added several price points and styles of designer lines. Do you want to be the General Motors of the designer business?

WATTENBERG: No, we have three divisions for different looks and customers. They also provide synergism because they are structured as three separate "companies" and the individual focus allows us to know about changes in one direction or another. We can put resources in natural shoulder if that's coming on strongly, or in young men's if that's happening.

MW: Are you deepening your involvement in sportswear as a hedge?

WATTENBERG: We plan to get into more sportswear. We learned a lot from our first year in the business. I think we jumped in too early because of demand. We're going to do it right in terms of product and delivery this year.

MW: Do stores still want coordinated packages or are they more comfortable with buying on their own?

WATTENBERG: I like the concept personally. The refinement of the concept is really Utopia. Now, the avant-garde guy who represents 1 or 2 percent of the business can put the looks together for a very specific customer type but most people who have the resources put the package together for them.

By refinement of the concept, I mean avoiding the situation where you put together slacks, tops, sweaters and jackets and vests and everything sells but the vests. What does the retailer, or the manufacturer for that matter, do with the vests? They don't go with anything now because you've sold the rest. ✷

Lion of Judah Award Speech — January 21, 1987

When Sy Syms called to tell me that the Israel Bond committee had bestowed this wonderful honor upon me, I was indeed quite surprised and flattered.

Being here at the Plaza is certainly a far cry from being smuggled through the German lines some 46 years ago. I was with my mother and aunt and we were trying to reach the Port of Marseille to board a ship to Spain and, eventually, the United States, to join my father Leon.

Although only about nine years old at the time, the memories of the Germans closing in on Paris and my life with the Free French Underground are still quite vivid in my mind.

I certainly remember the fear under Nazi rule. I certainly remember hearing about what the Germans had in store for any Jew that was captured. And I certainly remember wondering if we would ever get out of France alive.

I guess it is because of these very vivid memories of Jewish oppression that my abiding interest in the state of Israel has continued to grow over the years.

A strong Israel acts as a vanguard against prejudice, racial bias, and anti-Semitism. A strong Israel gives the United States a powerful ally in the Middle East. I feel a responsibility, as I'm sure you do, to help build a strong Israel. This is what an Israeli bond purchase is all about.

Much like the state of Israel, my mother, my aunt and I learned a long time ago that it's not how big the man in the fight, but rather how much fight there is in the man.

Thank you for joining us here tonight. And thank you for your continued care and concern. An Israeli bond purchase represents your best investment in freedom and democracy.

God bless you and may the New Year bring you and your families everything you ever hoped for. ✶

*This poem was written by Sheldon Fireman
on the occasion of my 60th birthday.*

Ode to Paul

Today your birthday has arrived,
And your enduring enthusiasm cannot be denied:
Tonight we rejoice for lots of great years –
Of laughter, love and occasional tears.

Can't truly say how many years old you are
One thing for sure, I'm younger by far.
So whether you're fifty-one or fifty-two
Happy Birthday – and by the way – I'm taller, too.

It's very special for us all to come
From hither and yon – toasting you as one;
And I wanted to write this ode to say,
You are my dearest friend in every way.

So as we wine and dine at Au Bar's awhile,
This poem is rooted in Bronx-type style;
For the friendship of Paul and me being cool –
Began in the halls of Creston Junior High School!

If it weren't for me having such a sense of humor
Staying your friend all these years would have just been a rumor.
See, I remember the times your *joie de vivre* was too much
    for others
But I felt from the beginning we were sort of like brothers.

How many people can you simply be with, be quiet
    and say nothing
That level of comfort is more than just something
And as I reminisce over our lives in this ode to you
I want you to know – you're one helluva Jew. →

I remember we had a number of things in common long ago
You had just come from France...and at English
    were a little slow
Given my stutter and difficulty "squeaking"
We were quite a team – relatively speaking!
The times we crashed costume balls and
    the Concorde Hotel Gate
How come we never came away with a foxy date?
Do you think it was because of your electric blue zoot suit?
I hate to tell you, but it made you look like a bit of a kook.

On the other hand, you sure wowed those gals
    on one New Year's Eve
When those Marines made eyes at them
    and began to bob and weave.
Your strength knocked them out and there was
    more than one moan
We won 'cause of you, and the blood on our clothes
    was not our own!

You were so smart in school, and a hero on the track team
Despite the fact you've been such a clutz,
    you've never been mean.
To the contrary, you're a man of much kindness and generosity
Though I must say, sometimes you're a bit of a curiosity!

Your family and friends join me tonight to share
Now just how much all of us deeply care.
You've achieved great success in your life and work
If only sometimes you weren't such a jerk!

Couldn't you spend more time on the golf course and just play?
I'd love to have time with you during the day.
We could chase chicks again and pretend we were
    boys of twenty
That would produce laughs a-plenty! →

Do you think we should reprint our cards from the past?
How many people know we were quite that suave and fast —
"Frenchie and Shelly...World's Greatest Lovers"
   the cards proclaimed
But they didn't work, never once did a
   Miss Subway by us get tamed!

But people over the years have learned a lot from you
I've never met anyone who could be so true blue —
Now we all know what an incredible pace you keep
Why not surprise us and slow down just long enough to sleep.

Imagine if you took time to listen to music or read some books —
Why it might even do something for your looks!!
Your creativity will shine through in anything you do
Can't wait to see what the next fifty years will have you pursue.
By the way Paul, this ode is not my only birthday gift to you
But it comes with a jacket from out of the blue —
As a towel boy on the DeWitt Clinton High School
   football team
You never got one...but richly deserve one it seems —

So with wishes for all things great and small
I say Happy Birthday to my dear friend Paul! ✴

designers

Charm and Talent

Were there only more fashion designers like Adolfo!

By Karen Alberg Grossman

With the opening of a new showroom and the launch of a new contemporary "Adolfo Jeune" collection for spring '09 (check out the fabulous unstructured sportcoat with stitched lapels and working buttonholes at $195 retail), Paul and Lee Wattenberg couldn't be happier. Nor could I, when I recently had the occasion to meet the designer himself: Adolfo Sardina. Born in Cuba in 1933, Adolfo immigrated to NYC in '48, became a citizen in '58 and served in the U.S. Navy. His design career began as an apprentice millinery designer at Bergdorf Goodman; from there he went to the Balenciaga Salon in Paris. He also apprenticed with Chanel, opened his own millinery salon in 1962, and then expanded into clothing. If you happened to have been in Manhattan on January 31, 1977, you might remember borough president Percy Sutton declaring an official "Adolfo Day." For more than 25 years, Adolfo dressed society ladies from C.Z. Guest and Betsy Bloomingdale to Jackie Kennedy and the Duchess of Windsor. He's received several Coty awards and today oversees numerous licenses.

Humble and gracious, Adolfo does not brag about his accomplishments, never even mentioning that a little red dress he designed for his friend Nancy Reagan is in the Smithsonian. Instead, he talks about menswear designers he currently admires, a list that includes Tom Ford, Marc Jacobs and Ralph Lauren.

But personally, he wears Adolfo. "My clothes from the past seem to last forever," he almost apologizes. Today, he's wearing a double-breasted blazer with slim gray trousers, a crisp checked shirt, and knit tie. "I sometimes shop at Bloomingdale's, Bergdorf or Selfridges. I like to dress quietly: a navy blazer with gray flannel

> ## "Men should dress discreetly, woman glamorously."
>
> *—Adolfo*

trousers will take you anywhere! And I've always believed that while women should dress glamorously, men should dress discreetly..."

Adolfo is Spanish on his father's side and Irish on his mother's (thus accounting for his natural blond hair). His family was in the sugar business in Cuba; some were lawyers. Most disappeared under Castro, and Adolfo was raised by an aunt and godfather. "They were like parents to me," he remembers, "but I came to the States on my own, and then moved to Paris on my own. My first job for Balenciaga was collecting pins from the floor..."

Had he not become a designer, he might have become a veterinarian as he truly loves dogs (he used to have four pugs). Another passion is reading, particularly biographies; he's currently reading about Marie-Thérèse-Charlotte, who was the only surviving daughter of Marie Antoinette. "I sometimes read fiction but I find biographies so much more interesting," he explains. "I learn so much."

Adolfo's favorite city is Manhattan, and his secret to health and longevity is that he walks everywhere. "He also knows a lot about wine," Paul Wattenberg adds with a smile.

His secret to happiness? Adolfo doesn't hesitate. "Each phase of my life has offered something wonderful. Each has a mystique. The trick is to appreciate where you are now." ∎

Adolfo (center) with Lee and Paul Wattenberg of Concorde Apparel

For designer news go to **www.MRketplace.com**

70 MR

MR, June 2008

MR *Article, June 2008:*
"Charm and Talent: Were there were only more fashion designers like Adolfo!"
By Karen Alberg Grossman

With the opening of a new showroom and the launch of a new contemporary "Adolfo Jeune" collection for spring '09 (check out the fabulous unstructured sportcoat with stitched lapels and working buttonholes at $195 retail), Paul and Lee Wattenberg couldn't be happier. Nor could I, when I recently had the occasion to meet the designer himself: Adolfo Sardina.

Born in Cuba in 1933, Adolfo immigrated to NYC in '48, became a citizen in '58 and served in the U.S. Navy. His design career began as an apprentice millinery designer at Bergdorf Goodman; from there he went to the Balenciaga salon in Paris. He also apprenticed with Chanel, opened his own millinery salon in 1962, and then expanded into clothing. If you happened to have been in Manhattan on January 31, 1977, you might remember borough president Percy Sutton declaring an official "Adolfo Day." For more than 25 years, Adolfo dressed society ladies from C.Z. Guest and Betsy Bloomingdale to Jackie Kennedy and the Duchess of Windsor. He's received several Coty awards and today oversees numerous licenses.

Humble and gracious, Adolfo does not brag about his accomplishments, never even mentioning that a little red dress he designed for his friend Nancy Reagan is in the Smithsonian. Instead, he talks about menswear designers he currently admires, a list that includes Tom Ford, Marc Jacobs and Ralph Lauren.

But personally, he wears Adolfo. "My clothes from the past seem to last forever," he almost apologizes. Today, he's wearing a double-breasted blazer with slim gray trousers, a crisp checked shirt, and knit tie. "I sometimes shop at Bloomingdales, Bergdorf or Selfridges. I like to dress quietly: a navy blazer →

with gray flannel trousers will take you anywhere! And I've always believed that while women should dress glamorously, men should dress discreetly."

Adolfo is Spanish on his father's side and Irish on his mother's (thus accounting for his natural blond hair). His family was in the sugar business in Cuba; some were lawyers. Most disappeared under Castro, and Adolfo was raised by an aunt and godfather. "They were like parents to me," he remembers, "but I came to the States on my own, and then moved to Paris on my own. My first job for Balenciaga was collecting pins from the floor..."

Had he not become a designer, he might have become a veterinarian as he truly loves dogs (he used to have four pugs). Another passion is reading, particularly biographies; he's currently reading about Marie-Thérèse-Charlotte, who was the only surviving daughter of Marie Antoinette. "I sometimes read fiction but I find biographies so much more interesting," he explains. "I learn so much."

Adolfo's favorite city is Manhattan, and his secret to health and longevity is that he walks everywhere. "He also knows a lot about wine," Paul Wattenberg adds with a smile.

His secret to happiness? Adolfo doesn't hesitate. "Each phase of my life has offered something wonderful. Each has a mystique. The trick is to appreciate where you are now." ✳

Linda and me at our 50th anniversary, 2010

FAMILY AND FRIENDS:
REFLECTIONS

Brenda and Carlin Axelrod
(Written in celebration of Paul's 75th birthday)
À l'occasion de 75eme anniversaire de Paul Wattenberg

Paul est un cher ami. Il montre toujours let souci véritable d'autres personnes.

Nous nous attendons à passer le temps avec lui, à cause des conversations stimulantes et accueillantes.

Tout le monde peut sentir sa chaleur. C'est notre bonne fortune d'avoir son amité.

Notre amour,
Brenda et Carlin Axelrod

Paul is a dear friend. He always shows true concern for other people.

We look forward to spending time with him because the conversation is stimulating and welcoming.

Everyone feels his warmth. We are very fortunate to have his friendship. ✱

With love,
Brenda and Carlin Axelrod

Note of Condolence:

My special cousin, Georges, passed away about one year ago. I am sad and regret that I did not finish my memoir so that he could read it. I hope Marink and Nataly will enjoy my memoirs. I feel, somehow, that Georges is us, in spirit, and reading these words.

Georges Bajczman

How did I meet Paul?

It was in Paris and I was six years old when I met him at his home (at this time they lived in Paris). I was with my parents. In fact, my father was the brother of Paul's mother. One time, we were with my cousin, Betty. Paul, Betty and I were at the back side of the textile shop, full of pieces of textiles and I remember that we liked to jump on them. Betty was older than us and she used to beat us a lot because we were just very excited.

War separated us. I stayed in France and Paul's family left to the United States of America. And so I don't have such memories of us when we were children. I remember that my aunt (Paul's mother) came back to France to visit us after the war and fortunately my mom and I were alive (my father died in the concentration camp during the war).

The second time I saw my family was in 1960. I went for the first time to New York to visit them. It was great because Paul never forgot his French (by the way, my English is just awful) and communication has always been possible between us.

Since then, I used to see Paul once a year and we feel very close. We like to be all together because he represents my whole family. I don't have other cousins actually with whom I keep in touch. Our children are almost the same age, our grandchildren, also. We know that there is a real familial link between all of us even if we don't live in the same country. In fact, I decided to buy an apartment in Miami because it was an opportunity for us to see each other often.

Hoping that our families stay as close as possible for the next generations. ✶

Georges

~~~~ **Pure Luck: The Extraordinary Life of Paul Wattenberg** ~~~~

Karen and Howard Blechman

Howard and I first met Linda and Paul when we lived in Forest Hills, New York. They ate every night at a restaurant at an hour that was way past our bedtime. They moved to Lake Success and we followed a few years later. Paul was always fun and filled with many stories of his past.

We have spent many vacations with Linda and Paul. Notably, one weekend in Vermont where Paul broke his leg in the parking lot while renting skis. He still was charming the entire weekend.

We have played golf and after many "Paul's" have finally finished the round.

We have shared Paris with Paul and heard many tales of his childhood. It's amazing how he overcame all his troubles and became a great success in business as well as a wonderful father and grandfather.

Paul is a very special person. He's kind and feels great empathy for people in need. He is always available to listen to a friend's troubles and try to help.

He is a man for all seasons. ✱

~~~ **268** ~~~

Stuart and Sylvia Cooper

I met Paul 40 years ago. I talk to him at least five times a week. We are of the same personality. He is a very hard-working man. He is a wonderful husband, father and grandfather. I remember the stories of how he and his family were in Europe and how they all suffered. He is a special person. He is humble, compassionate and good-natured. I remember his mother very well. She could not have had a better son. He is a compulsive worker. Paul is very special to me because of his compassion, sincerity and a feeling if you ever needed a friend, he would always be there.

Stuart Cooper

Paul is all the wonderful things that my husband has written. I feel as he does.

I also recall all the times we vacationed, partied, celebrated and cried together. Paul has been there for us at all times and I truly cherish him and Linda. ✦

Sylvia Cooper

Murray Eisen

Paul has been my very close and dear friend for almost 60 years. We have never had a cross word or misunderstanding and we never will.

Paul is a very special person and as good a friend as I will ever have. If Paul is your friend, you have a friend for life.

Some of my memories are very special. Perhaps the most special is the way we first met. It was December, college break, and I had driven to Miami Beach, as did most of my friends and classmates in New York University. I shared my annual drive to South Beach with Herb Taub, who usually spent most of his Christmas break at the racetrack (losing our meager funds) rather than enjoying the beach. Just as we were getting ready to leave and drive back up to New York (before Herb even lost our gas money), I was approached on the beach with what sounded like a vacation-saving request. A fraternity friend said, "Murray, do you know this French guy from the Bronx, his name is Paul Wattenberg?"

He was surprised to hear that I didn't know him because he went on to say, "He has been up and down the beach asking everyone from school if anyone knows if there is a hotel room available. Since Herb has not been doing well at Hialeah and you are planning to drive home, why not get another bed in your room and Paul will share the expenses and you guys can stay until after New Year's?"

It sounded like a great idea, except for the fact that the room was so small to begin with that, when the third bed was added, the room became almost one large bed. As you opened the door, you stepped onto the bed and walked over whomever was in it. Remembering who was in the beds and how often the guests and overnight visitors changed made every night an adventure. →

From the day Paul moved into our room, our hotel room and discussions about the nightly comings and goings kept everyone on the beach laughing and guessing every morning.

Paul and I became the closest of friends when we returned to New York. Another book could be written about growing up on the Grand Concourse with Shelly Fireman, Lenny Lauren and the whole cast of characters that populated our lives. These are memories of the beautiful Bronx in another place, another time.

More Christmas Florida trips were memorable. In fact, we spent much of the year planning the annual Christmas drive to South Beach. In the early 1950's, people who wanted their cars driven to Florida would advertise in the New York Times and in our college newspaper. Paul and I would always try to find a big convertible (Lincoln or Cadillac) and someone who was not in a particular rush to have his car reach South Florida.

I know Paul has special memories of those college trips over Christmas breaks and the Fairfax and Seacomber Surfcomber Hotels. (These memories are RRR – Triple R – rated and not printable. Since I know there should be a movie about Paul, his life and family, when this movie, "The Frenchman," is made, we definitely want to get at least a PG rating.)

I will never forget his coming to me and telling me, "I met the girl I'm going to marry. She is the love of my life and we met at the Lake Tarleton Club, so she must be very rich."

After college, our friendship grew and our families became very close. My memory of Lee's bris in Paul and Linda's Forest Hills apartment house's recreation room is as clear as if I were there last night, since I was the "Kohan" (the High Priest needed in ancient times at the ceremony.)

Our families spent every summer together at the Beach Clubs, both in Atlantic Beach and Lido Beach, where we   →

shared cabanas and shared the trials and tribulations of raising our children.

Listening to the sounds of the seagulls and the crashing of the waves, one would always hear another new sea-and-surf sound provided all day long by Linda, usually in a high-pitched tone, "Paul, where is Lee?!!"

Needless to say, I will always thank Linda's acting like "Dr. Phil"when Roberta and I had a real issue. (Although it loomed large at the time, I can't even remember what it was about.) Linda told Roberta that she was cooking dinner, and Paul told me the same thing. We both walked in and, during that most memorable evening, Roberta and I found each other again. All it took was a little conversation, along with Linda and Paul helping us to realize that nothing was as important as staying together, no matter our issues. They were surely right. After we got back together, we had Felicia, Debbi, Richard, and seven precious grandchildren.

Sadly, I lost Roberta after 40 beautiful years together.

Roberta and I were there when Lee, Debbie, and Wendy were born. I have beautiful memories of Bar Mitzvahs, Bat Mitzvahs, weddings, births of grandchildren and all the precious moments our families shared together.

We were really one family and I know how proud Roberta would be to see little Lee, Debbie, and Wendy today. Wendy, a power at Saks Fifth Avenue. Dr. Debbie Wattenberg, whom I never miss on NBC. Lee, helping to bring Adolfo to another level (and patiently waiting for Paul to retire!)

Paul's relationship with his father and mother was a beautiful and special part of his life and I shared it with him.

During our NYU days, I enjoyed visiting Paul at Leon of Paris's loft on Union Square and watching how closely Paul, his father, and his mother worked together to grow the business into what it is today. They had a work ethic that is rarely →

seen. I never saw an issue or misunderstanding as they all worked together with the same goals and aspirations.

Paul tragically lost his parents at an early age. I suffered with him during the sad and long illness of his mother, as Paul and Linda shared with me the loss of my wife, Roberta.

Paul and I and our families had a circle of friends and we usually took our vacations together. I could probably write a book about those years. Sylvia and Stuart Cooper, Shelly and Marilyn Fireman (one of our Bronx success stories), Sid and Judy Myers, Howard and Harriet Davis, Beverly and Ira Howard, Howie Dryer, Paul Jane, Shirley and Morty Spar, and so many others.

These are just some of the memories of Paul, his life and his loved ones, that I will hold onto always and that have helped to make my life so rich and full of laughter. Here's to many more moments of wonderful adventures for Paul and his family, and for all of us together, side-by-side. ✴

Philip Elkus

My life with Paul Wattenberg –

We date back to more than a half century ago, when Paul made his first road/sales trip to Detroit. I vividly recall when he walked into our store, Todd's, in downtown Detroit. What I remember is how much he looked like his father...a living clone!

Actually, our fathers did business together, and the two of us just carried on. That journey together took us from his first loft on Fifth Avenue to his move to 23rd Street, then on to 1290 Avenue of the Americas, then to his present location on 56th Street.

What a journey that was, no, *is*!

Going back to that Fifth Avenue loft, what a madhouse that was! Small, people on top of each other, phones ringing, samples, swatches piled all over the place, Eve London trying to make sense of it all, trying to tie up the sales area while Paul's mother carefully watched over and controlled the cutting room.

Then the BIG move to 23rd Street. Leon of Paris had arrived, the Full Monty: sales office, cutting room and factory! I remember the grand opening. Linda had decorated the showroom, it was spectacular! Paul's mother had her own office overseeing the cutting room, and a completely new factory with sparkling new machinery on the floor below.

It was during that time that one of Paul's contemporaries said to me, "I don't know about the rest of us, but as the clothing business consolidates, Paul will be the last man standing!" How true those words were! When Paul made his first trip to Detroit, Leon of Paris was, at best, a third-tier supplier. The leader in that space of the menswear business was Blankson Clothes, followed by Meilman & Maged and Belmont Clothes. Then there was a third group of a dozen manufacturers, including Leon of Paris, all clambering for position. Paul, →

indeed, was the survivor, leaving all of his contemporaries recorded in history books.

What were Paul's great survival attributes? He is very, very talented, but his perseverance outshines them all. Once on a case, there is absolutely no letting up. Tie that up with his sales ability...nothing makes him happier than making a sale, and he could have been a survivor anyhow. But add to that his remarkable sense of style, his ability to pick patterns, to jump on color trends, to select fabrics, to promote a style trend...and you have that unique winning combination that has made Paul a legend in his own time.

It was during the time of the 23rd Street location that one of Paul's best moves took place. Teaming up with Adolfo...a combination that turned out to be the best investment ever for Paul. I remember once, when Paul picked me up at the airport and took an extra detour to the city, just to pass a huge Adolfo billboard near the Midtown Tunnel. The public relations work done that first year was extraordinary. The Adolfo label became a leading property for the Saks's of the world.

It was during this era that we would work together on "Cleanout Sessions." We would start at the shipping area around 4 p.m. and the two of us would bargain, discuss, agree and disagree on the price of all the goods on hand. I'd split up the various buys into my 3 different operations (The Warehouse, our 4-Day Store and Baron's). Paul and I would dance up and down the loft for a couple of hours, then have dinner and call it a day, or rather, a night.

After the 23rd Street factory showroom became obsolete, Paul moved his factory to Brooklyn and his office to 1290 Avenue of the Americas, the Sperry-Rand Building. By this time, Leon of Paris had elaborate offices and a basketful of divisions. John Hampton and Caravelle are two of the half-dozen that come to mind. →

Moving on to the Sperry-Rand Building, our "Cleanout Sessions" (when I would clear out all his odds and ends, credit holds, over cuts, etc.) was split between his two locations: Brooklyn operation and his Caravelle operation. It wasn't as much fun, too many locations, and much too much goods. But we carried on!

Then the industry had its major consolidation. The Brooklyn factory couldn't compete with the international market, and it...and the rest of the business collapsed. But not Paul.

Paul started to import from China directly, and I was honored to be able to assist him with those first couple of shipments. Those first few shipments were so successful that, along with his son Lee, we were able to regenerate his business and to build what it is today – a major player in the menswear market.

So much for the business side. I remember when we first met Linda. My wife Estelle and I were at Rubins, a famous and well-regarded deli near the Plaza Hotel. Sitting at a table not far from us were Linda, Paul and a half dozen other couples, all in tuxes and formalwear. And what were they doing? It was their Saturday night special. They'd crash parties at the Plaza Hotel, attending the dessert/dancing portion of the parties. What fun...and better yet, at no cost!

There was also a 'game' that I would play with Paul. I'd try not to tell him I would be coming to New York and see how long it would take him to track me down. I recall once, Estelle and I had just checked in our room, hadn't even started to unpack, and Estelle asked me if I had contacted Paul. She was amazed I hadn't and asked me, "Why not?" My response was, "I don't know how he knows, but..." just then the phone rang. Yes, it was Paul!

Another time while at the MAGIC Show in San Diego, we had decided to make a mini-vacation out of it and rented a condo at La Costa with another couple, the Waldsteins. →

Because it was a vacation and we didn't want to mix the Waldsteins with the Wattenbergs, and because La Costa was 30 miles
from the MAGIC convention center, we thought we'd be iso-
lated from Paul. So who winds up with the condo next door?
Paul and Linda! Turned out the mix was nothing but fun!

I had my own schtick; I tried to keep my personal life separate from my business. So when our first son, Bill, was Bar
Mitzvah'd, we did not invite any guests that were connected to
the clothing business. But a week later, Sonny Friedman, one
of our competitors in Detroit, had his son Bar Mitzvah'd, and
Linda and Paul attended. While they were in Detroit, Paul and
Linda were able to spend an afternoon with us at our home
where they met our four sons. Paul asked Bill when he was
going to be Bar Mitzvah'd, and Bill told him it was "last
week." To say the least, Paul was hurt that he and Linda hadn't
been invited. I tried to explain, but you know Paul. He isn't
too receptive to a counter explanation...and he insisted upon
being invited to Larry's Bar Mitzvah three years later.

Three years later, I still didn't want to invite any business
friends and didn't send the Wattenbergs an invitation. But on
the Tuesday before Larry's Bar Mitzvah, the phone rang about
9 p.m. and it was Paul! And I just knew that somehow, somewhere, Paul found out about Larry's Bar Mitzvah, but I still
wasn't going to say anything. So the call went on and on and
on and on, finally Paul said he's arriving in Detroit Friday and
leaving Saturday late afternoon. He did attend the actual Bar
Mitzvah and left for the airport shortly afterwards. He certainly
one-upped me on that time.

So I had to break down and include my business friends,
most especially the Wattenbergs, thereafter, for Bob and
David's Bar Mitzvahs. For truth to tell, they had become far
more than just business friends, but almost family. →

Which brings up another of Paul's endearing traits, his complete and total devotion to his family. Pure and simple, family means more to him than anything else. I've seen him, time and time again, go far above the call of duty for his far-flung family.

My wife Estelle, Linda, Paul and I have probably had a thousand meals together from New York to California. From Michigan to Florida, even in Europe – but one extraordinary meal remains most noteworthy. We sat down at the Trattoria del Artes to have our first meal there together (we are both in-vestors in the restaurant). Just as we started to order, Shelly Fireman, the owner, walked in along with his wife and son, spotted us, and invited the four of us to join them. The seven of us sat down to, absolutely, the greatest meal ever. Shelly did all the ordering and the staff just kept bringing dishes out of the kitchen. It was fabulous. Just as we finished with one or two plates, then another would come. Then the dessert – I won't even mention about that, except for the encore – a cookie the size of a huge dinner plate with a special liqueur. Shelly broke the cookie into pieces, dipped it into the liqueur and voilà! But then the most remarkable of all...when the bill arrived for all seven of us, Shelly handed it over to Paul...and Paul paid it. I still can't get over that one. The next day, when I asked Paul the whys and what-fors, he just simply said, "That's Shelly."

This essay more or less summarizes over 50 years of doing business with Paul; socializing with Linda and Paul; millions of phone calls (usually too late at night); of investing with and alongside Paul; of each of us supporting the other during peri-ods of highs and lows.

Let's put it all together into one single sentence: "Paul has put a lot of Style in our Life...and a lot of Life in our Style. ✷

Sheldon Fireman

I have a very clear vision of Paul as a youth. I can see him now: a bright-eyed, highly energetic, handsome blond-haired young man, blessed with genuine speed and strength, if not, to be perfectly frank, a natural grace. Paul was probably stronger, and much faster than I was, and despite his potentially intimidating gifts, he was never anything but the most naturally gentle, happy-go-lucky guy. I can't remember ever seeing Paul's face filled with anger. I don't think real anger 'computes' with him. Paul was always easy to get along with, but occasionally, his enthusiasm and drive could lead him to display a slightly 'show-offy' quality that may not have been appreciated by the youth of that day, who were for the most part less ambitious than Paul and probably didn't quite understand him.

As I'm writing this, I close my eyes and try to picture all of it as it was. I am not going to tell you funny or silly experiences because we all have funny and silly experiences. I will say that Paul always handled a situation with grace and generosity even when the joke was on him. Interesting observations come to mind, ones I have probably never articulated to myself, let alone Paul. Paul's youth was marked by an ability to overcome tremendous obstacles, which I greatly admired. There are the obvious examples, the terrible experience in Europe, learning a new language, but thinking back, I find myself dwelling on the smaller hurdles. One handicap he may have had as a very young man is that he didn't come from a background of baseball or football, so his natural athletic abilities didn't show up immediately in the neighborhood. He was the Frenchman, not the guy who could hit a stickball or catch a baseball. Yet I never once saw that upset him or make him doubt himself. →

Paul was above all a tremendously respectful young man. Respectful of all people, particularly his family. He was just that kind of a wonderful son. When I think about it today, you probably couldn't find anybody better. At times maybe he was even too good a son, and brother, because while his devotion to others made for the wonderful character that he has, it also comes along with its own handicaps. He was a devoted son, gosh was he devoted. He was devoted even in situations that didn't call for devotion except in his wonderful value system. You have to admire how he got those values. Did he learn them at home? Or was it just his natural instinct as a human being? I don't know the answer, I'm just glad it's the case.

Obviously Paul struggled in coming to this country. He won the French medal in school, but there he did come with an advantage. Despite his having to readjust to a new language and culture Paul was always a good student, an attentive student who truly grasped the information he was taught. I find it sad that life forced him, for the sake of his family, to enter the business world long before he was ready and long before he had the opportunity to discover all the intellectual opportunities that he could have probably mastered and enjoyed to this day. But such was the nature of Paul's devotion. A moment suddenly comes to mind. Paul and I were driving over the Triboro bridge, he had a fancy car at the time, must've been in the university or last year of high school. I remember his telling me how good he was on certain tests, and that a professor had told him he had great aptitude in learning, probably more so than in business. I'm not knocking his business sense just feeling sorry because I think he would have been a great scholar and a great teacher. I think he would have enjoyed that tremendously. But things didn't go that way. His father died at a young age. He was driven from a depression, escaping from a horrible situation in Europe. And he was driven by the American dream at the →

time, the dream for the material success. He was one of those ambitious people, he ran fast, and I don't mean literally ran, to achieve wonderful success and all the pleasant little bonuses such as accolades from his peers. Whether the American dream is a good dream or a bad dream, I don't know. But I know that I love Paul. I respect him. I feel that I wish I could wave the magic wand and give him time to read all the books he could. I also wish he would stop feeling the material of my jackets which he's done all my life. Because I'm sure he puts a price on how much I paid for the jacket, or more likely, how much I overpaid for the jacket.

While Paul may have looked extrinsically affluent to some people because he wore nice clothes, his father owned a Cadillac, and he lived on the Grand Concourse with a step down living room, in truth, he was far from wealthy and often had to struggle. Closing my eyes, I can see Paul's father's face perfectly – a nice upbeat man with a delightful smile who always seemed happy. I think Paul takes after his father tremendously in this regard. But Paul's love for his mother trumped all. He treated her with such respect and honor and to this day has never uttered a negative word about her, only that she was a wonderful mother whom he loved and respected. I always wondered where that came from, that unbelievable capacity for love. Was that hardwired in 'the computer?' Was he taught that at home by his family? In either event it's an amazing thing. He honored her forever. Many times he gave up things in order to do for her and looking back, I can certainly say it wasn't the wrong thing to do.

So there we have ambition, drive, intelligence, enthusiasm, a general sense of niceness, devotion, loyalty...easy to see that with those qualities you can achieve many things and he surely has. He's had to give up some things too. I have to say that when I look at his life and what he's contributed to society, →

to his family, and to his friends, he has probably contributed more than he receives. Paul probably got the short end of the stick. Except I don't think he feels that or even sees it that way. Because love and loyalty are Paul's nature. Bless him for it.

I asked Paul over and over what the purpose of the book is? Is it a book to read to your family about your life? Is it a real story? Is it a make-believe story? Is it a dream of what you would like to have been or how you would like to be remembered? I never got a clear answer from him so all I can do here is to tell the truth. To his children, grandchildren, great grandchildren and great-great grandchildren: Paul was and is a wonderfully decent man who gave more than he got. Although he'll tell you he got a lot. When you think about him alive or long gone, know that he was by nature a *contributor* to other people's lives, to his family, and should be recognized and remembered for that. He contributed to the world around him. He brought better things to people. I'm proud to say that Paul has been my friend since as long as I've had friends. And I'm not too proud to say that he has much more tolerance and patience for the human condition than I could ever have and I admire him for that. I admire him and I love him. ✶

Stuart Golden

I worked for Paul for 25 years, since 1971, and we became
best friends. How hard he worked. One time when I was
working for him – selling together, designing fabrics, doing
garment models – we were together for 16 hours. I live in
Brooklyn, about an hour's train ride home. By the time I got
home, it was 11:30 at night. I was very tired. I walked in the
house and the phone was ringing. I answered. Who was it?
Paul Wattenberg! "I have to ask you one more question," he
said. After 16 hours!

Paul lived in Great Neck. Now I was driving into Manhattan, because after three years, I was making a little more money,
so I could pay for my parking and actually drive to work at 46
West 23rd Street, between 5th and 6th Avenues. We had another
16 hour day. He said, "Stuart, I'll take you to Sarge's Deli for
some dinner." After dinner, he said, "You take the Belt Parkway
home, don't you?" I said yes. He said, "On the way home, you
can drop me off." Now, I said, "Paul, I go on the Belt Parkway
West and you go on the Belt Parkway East, which is about 40
miles out of my way – through the Queens-Midtown Tunnel,
the LIE to exit 33, Great Neck. Then I take the Belt Parkway
40 miles west to go to Brooklyn." So it was an extra 80 miles to
take him home and for me to get home. And that's Paul. I got
home and the phone rang and guess who it was? Paul. "I have
to ask you a question," he said.

We were going to an account – the House of Cromwell –
and I was carrying the 100 lbs. garment bag, which looks like a
body bag. He was 10 feet ahead of me, running for cabs, yelling
back at me, "Where are you already?" That's Paul!

I love the man because he is the most knowledgeable person I ever met. If you needed a doctor, he was a doctor. →

(He knew everything about the medical field.) Besides being a doctor of swatchology, he really is a doctor of everything about life. Paul was always a very special person. He taught me everything I know about the menswear industry and gave me my start to being a very successful person.

About five or six years after I started working for the company, they needed to lay off people and management wanted to lay me off. Paul said, "What, are you crazy? This is the best guy we've got. He's the upcoming Mickey Mantle of the industry." I was about 28 at the time. I worked with him for another 15 years after that.

He was so special that he lit candles at both my children's Bar and Bat Mitzvahs.

The man is a god to me – very well-respected. I am sorry I am not working with him today. ✶

Morty Howard

There are several stories that best describe Paul and his persona. I believe this one defines him and what drives him through life.

Paul started to learn golf later on in his mature life. This is very difficult. Golf, as we all realize, is very hard to master, particularly when you do not take to it early in your teens or twenties. Paul took lessons and he practiced and practiced constantly. After a few years, he asked me to play with him. Quote: "Can I join you?" Kiddingly, I said, "Paul, I'm sorry, our threesome is all filled. There isn't any room for you."

He was a little upset. However, we knew he wasn't ready for my group and he would only be intimidated. A year later, I drew Paul as my partner in our yearly USA Tournament. He was thrilled! He went around the club, screaming, "I drew Morty Howard as my partner! I drew the champ. We are going to do good!"

Well, for the first ten holes, I did not do too good. Then on the eleventh hole, our toughest par three, Paul put his tee shot on the green and then sunk the putt for a natural birdie. He looked at me and with his cutest smile said, "So, *schtarka*. When do you plan to help our team? I can't do this alone!"

Such *joie de vivre*. His total commitment and dedication to play well is, once again, a true sign of Paul's will to do the best he can in whatever he does. He will always have my admiration and respect for being an all-around father, grandfather, and friend. ✷

With much affection,
Morty Howard

Steven Lossing

Paul Wattenberg is one of the most remarkable individuals I have had the pleasure to meet in my 20-plus years in this industry. He is an incredible salesman with an uncanny ability not to hear the word "no" – especially from retailers. He is responsible for one of the most memorable dinners of my life – he somehow convinced the S&W Steakhouse at the Wynn hotel in Las Vegas to allow a karaoke machine to be brought into the restaurant so that he could sing a Frank Sinatra duet with a table full of JCPenney associates. I'm quite sure that had never been done before and, after our performance, will never be done again!

Paul's passion and enthusiasm for the product and the business are infectious. He has an incredible energy level and work ethic than many executives half his age would find difficult to match. Paul has a lot of remarkable qualities, but it's his love for life and for his wonderful family that I have always admired the most. His life story, like the man himself, is truly remarkable. I consider myself lucky to not only have the opportunity to work with Paul as a business associate, but to be able to call him a friend. Paul, thanks for the friendship, the amazing memories so far and for the ones yet to come. ✸

Regards,
Steve

Sid Myers

I'm sure many people will write about Paul's devotion to his family, his unquestioned loyalty to friends, his caring, sympathy and contributions to many Jewish causes.

To me, however, the strength of Paul's character is his unflagging optimism and resolute courage in the face of trial. This quality in my opinion comes from his mother. During the war, she took her young son Paul, and with grit and guts traveled with him through France with the Nazis hard on their heels. One step ahead of certain death, she made her way through hostile territory and fought her way to freedom in the United States.

This certainly had a profound effect on Paul. I am truly amazed at his resilience when life throws him a curve ball. It is easy to be a great guy when you're riding high, but the true test of character comes forth when things are darkest, whether in business or family life. Paul certainly has proved to me that he has the tenacity to pass that test with courage and strength of purpose.

I am proud to be his friend, and promise to honor the pact we made to be friends until our hundred and twentieth year (minus one). May the next 44 years be full of joy, health and *mazel* for you. ✷

I love you.
Sid Myers

Midge Rosenberg

Dear Debbie, Wendy and Lee,

I know your parents for better than forty years and we have retained a wonderful friendship.

The fondest thoughts I have about Paul are – he is a great friend but more important – he is a fabulous family man. My daughter Laurie and his daughter Debbie have been best friends since they were very young girls. When I lost my husband, Laurie was inconsolable and Paul was fantastic to her. She will never forget it and neither will I.

Paul is a self-made man and, with all the success he has had in his life, his attitude about family is the absolute shining star as far as I am concerned. It's all about his wife, children and, of course, the greatest dividends, his *grandchildren*. ✶

Midge Rosenberg

Interviews with Paul and Linda Wattenberg
were conducted and edited
by Teri Friedman, PhD
at their home in New York City,
between 2006 and 2010.

CPSIA information can be obtained at www.ICGtesting.com
Printed in the USA
BVOW081159231012

303724BV00001B/5/P